THIS GREAT
salvation

UNMERITED FAVOR, UNMATCHED JOY

C.J. MAHANEY AND ROBIN BOISVERT

Executive Editor: Greg Somerville

SOVEREIGN GRACE™ MINISTRIES
The Pursuit *of* Godliness Series

Sovereign Grace Media is a division of Sovereign Grace Ministries, which serves a growing network of local churches in the United States and abroad. For information about the ministry or for permission to reproduce portions of this book, please contact us.

Sovereign Grace Ministries
7505 Muncaster Mill Road
Gaithersburg, MD 20877

301-330-7400
fax: 301-948-7833
info@sovgracemin.org
www.sovereigngraceministries.org

Authors: C.J. Mahaney and Robin Boisvert
Cover design: Gallison Design (www.gallisondesign.com)
Book layout: Carl Mahler

ISBN 1-881039-01-3

Printed in the United States of America

0603

CONTENTS

How to Use This Book   v

Foreword   vii

CHAPTER ONE
This Great Salvation   C.J. Mahaney   1

CHAPTER TWO
Does Anyone Believe in Sin? Robin Boisvert   13

CHAPTER THREE
The Holiness of God   Robin Boisvert   25

CHAPTER FOUR
The Wrath of God   C.J. Mahaney   37

CHAPTER FIVE
Justified by Christ   C.J. Mahaney   49

CHAPTER SIX
The Fruits of Justification (I)   Robin Boisvert   59

CHAPTER SEVEN
The Fruits of Justification (II) Robin Boisvert   73

Notes   90

HOW TO USE THIS BOOK

This Great Salvation, like each book in the Pursuit of Godliness series, is designed for group and individual use. The series is the logical outgrowth of four deeply held convictions:

■ The Bible is our infallible standard for faith, doctrine, and practice. Those who resist its authority will be blown off course by their own feelings and cultural trends.

■ Knowledge without application is lifeless. In order to be transformed, we must apply and practice the truth of God's Word in daily life.

■ Application of these principles is impossible apart from the Holy Spirit. While we must participate in change, he is the source of our power.

■ The church is God's intended context for change. God never intended for us to live isolated from or independent of other Christians. Through committed participation in the local church, we find instruction, encouragement, correction, and opportunities to press on toward maturity in Christ.

As you work through these pages, we trust each of these foundational convictions will be reinforced in your heart.

With the possible exception of the "Group Discussion" questions, the format of this book is equally suited for individuals and small groups. A variety of different elements have been included to make each chapter as interesting and helpful as possible. For those of you who can't get enough of a particular topic, we've listed at the end of each chapter one or more additional books that will help you grow in the Lord.

While you are encouraged to experiment in your use of this book, group discussion will be better served when members work through the material in advance. And remember that you're not going through this book alone. The Holy Spirit is your tutor. With his help, this book has the potential to change your life.

FOREWORD

It hardly needs to be stated that in order to promote passionate devotion to Jesus Christ, pastoral leaders ought to encourage the study of doctrine. If there has been one thought that has driven and guided the production of this book, it is that doctrine matters. How can we worship and serve a God we are ignorant of, or worse yet, one of our own making? Doctrine has not only inspired heartfelt love for God, but it has served as the moral compass of the Church throughout her history. Believing what is true about God leads to practicing what is acceptable before God.

We need to consider the question asked by the author of Hebrews: "How shall we escape if we ignore such a great salvation?" (2:3). Our gracious God has supplied us with a great salvation—full, free, and finished. There really is no excuse for neglect of all God has done for us. "His divine power has given us everything we need for life and godliness through our knowledge of him who called us by his own glory and goodness" (2Pe 1:3).

Coming to an awareness of this is one thing. Entering into the experience of it is quite another. Our hope is that a user-friendly format will make studying doctrine more fulfilling and less daunting. We (the authors) are little more than beginners ourselves in this adventure. That's why the recommended reading at the close of each chapter may be the most valuable part of the book. But if our experience be limited, it has been enough to forever change the way we think and live. We have also had the added advantage of preaching and teaching this material and seeing it radically affect those we are privileged to serve in pastoral ministry.

This great salvation has been changing lives profoundly, dramatically, and consistently since the gospel was first proclaimed. For more of the same to occur through the study of this book would, for us, be very gratifying.

Our thanks to Greg Somerville for his editorial expertise and tireless efforts in the production of this book. In addition, we express our thanks to production coordinator Beth Kelley and graphic designer Carl Mahler for the contribution of their special talents. Working with them as a team has been very satisfying.

Finally, we would like to dedicate this book to our wives and best friends, Carolyn Mahaney and Clara Boisvert, who have helped us translate doctrine into life. They have our deepest admiration.

— **C.J. Mahaney and Robin Boisvert**

CHAPTER ONE

THIS GREAT SALVATION

C.J. MAHANEY

Meditate on Hebrews 10:19-24. What gives us the confidence to stand in God's holy presence?

The week before I was scheduled to speak at a marriage retreat, my wife Carolyn mentioned a specific deficiency in our relationship. Actually, it was my own selfishness. I had become increasingly preoccupied with my studies and had failed to spend time with her in meaningful communication. Still, I felt so pressured to complete preparations for the retreat and the following Sunday message that I didn't respond or change. I thought I had a legitimate excuse.

But in the midst of my preparations, as I was developing the point that selfishness is a root problem in many marriages, I felt the Holy Spirit broadside me with all the force of Nathan's prophecy to King David: "Thou art the man!" My guilt was obvious. So I called Carolyn immediately to ask for her forgiveness. As I expected, she forgave me without hesitation. (Being married to me has given her lots of practice in that area.)

As I began to study again, though, I experienced the painful and all too familiar reality of accusation. An insistent thought interrupted my efforts: "What qualifies you to teach about marital intimacy in light of the fact that you've violated what you will be teaching? You even violated it while you were *preparing* it!"

I had no problem identifying the source of the guilt that threatened to paralyze me. The challenge was, how do I shake it?

Another scenario had confronted me just a week or two before. Apparently a number of the appliances in my home had conspired to break down simultaneously.

> **❝** A wise man has said that your Christian life is like a three-legged stool. The legs are doctrine, experience, and practice. In recent years many Christian people have not kept these three together.[1] **❞**
>
> — J.I. Packer

(Have you noticed how that happens? Why can't things break individually, in a sequence you can handle?) The vacuum cleaner broke. The microwave broke—a major disaster in my home. I have a hard time waiting 15 *seconds* for the microwave to nuke my food. Wait 15 minutes for the oven? No chance! In addition, it appeared that our heat pump was malfunctioning when we received our electric bill for twice the normal amount.

Before the week ended I faced one final surprise. Carolyn had gotten up early to jog. After stepping out of the house, she came back in and asked calmly, "Where's the car?" I just looked at her, unsure how to answer. *Where's the car?* I thought to myself. *It's in the driveway. That's where we put cars.* But it wasn't in the driveway. I waited a full 45 minutes before calling the authorities, fully expecting one of my friends to call and confess that it was a practical joke. The phone never rang. Later that day the police found my abandoned car miles away, intact except for the wheels. Stolen right out of my driveway!

How are we to respond to a nagging sense of guilt (accusation), combined with difficult and confusing circumstances (adversity)? You've probably experienced similar if not more serious things yourself. Too often we are more aware of accusations than we are of God's grace; we're perplexed, even bitter during adversity rather than certain of God's sovereignty.

Please take a moment now to read Romans 8:28-39, before you proceed any further with this chapter. As incredible as it may seem, a solid grasp of the truths contained in these twelve verses will enable you to respond with a convincing "Yes!" to each of the questions in the box to the left. There's no more effective response to accusation and adversity than this magnificent section of Scripture.

For Further Study: If ever anyone had a right to complain about life's troubles, it was Job. Contrast his attitude before his revelation of God's sovereignty (Job 19:1-21) and after (Job 42:1-6).

---

1 For each of the questions below, put an "X" on that part of the scale that most accurately reflects your current condition.

❑ Are you secure—not merely aware of, but consistently secure—in God's love for you? Are you amazed by God's grace?

◄ - ►

No   Somewhat   Yes

❑ Are you typically able to resist doubts and depression when experiencing trials?

◄ - ►

No   Somewhat   Yes

Do You Know?

Two of the verses in our passage from Romans would qualify for any list of "Most Quoted" sections of the Bible:

And we know that in all things God works for the good of those who love him, who have been called according to his purpose. (v. 28)

What, then, shall we say in response to this? If God is for us, who can be against us? (v.31)

But let me submit something for your consideration. Too often I think we try to exhort and encourage each other with these verses without understanding the content of the two verses in between. It's a futile attempt, for unless we understand the context provided in verses 29 and 30, we can't fully appreciate the promises in verses 28, 31, and the passage that follows. Take a close look at these two pivotal verses:

For those God foreknew he also *predestined* to be conformed to the likeness of his Son, that he might be the firstborn among many brothers. And those he predestined, he also *called;* those he called, he also *justified;* those he justified, he also *glorified.* (v.29-30)

If you had shown up at my house on the day my car was stolen and my microwave was malfunctioning, you could have legitimately counseled me to believe that "all things work together for the good." I hope I would have responded to this biblical truth. Likewise, you could have exhorted me to reject the guilt that remained after I asked Carolyn's forgiveness by reminding me, "If God is for us, who can be against us? Who will bring any charge against those whom God has chosen? It is God who justifies." Again, I couldn't dispute the accuracy of this truth. But if not understood in context, these promises can do no more than bring temporary change or relief. Their effectiveness is limited until we understand the doctrines contained in verses 29 and 30.

As we read Romans 8:28-39, it's clear that Paul was convinced of the things he wrote. He *knew* that all things were working together for good in his life, despite trials and suffering of a nature that we'll never encounter. (Paul defined "good" not in terms of personal pleasure and pros-

> ❝ You have heard the adage, 'Ignorance is the mother of superstition.' Unfortunately, many people's theology is the crystallizing of ignorance more than the systematizing of God's revelation. They wander about in the theological dark, formulating doctrines that belong in the world of witch doctors. Therefore, we need to say more than that everyone has a theology when asked, Why theology? We need to distinguish between right theology and wrong theology. For theology is like a backbone. Right theology will have you walking straight and fit. Wrong theology will have you hunchbacked and paralyzed.[2] ❞
>
> — James Cantelon

For Further Study:
How could the man who lived through the experiences recorded in 2 Corinthians 11:23-33 write Romans 15:13?

3

perity, but being conformed to the image of Christ.) He *knew* that God had justified him even when he experienced accusation. He *knew* that nothing—adversity, persecution, accusation, demonic harassment, or even death itself—could separate him from the love of Christ (v.35). What gave him such confidence and assurance? It was his intimate familiarity with these five crucial doctrines: foreknowledge, predestination, calling, justification, and glorification.

That same degree of conviction and faith will fill you as you meditate on the content of verses 29 and 30. You will be able to respond with confidence, *"It is God who justifies,"* whenever the accusations occur. You will be able to say with certainty, *"All things are working together for good in my life,"* even though you may be experiencing circumstances that appear confusing, perplexing, and even contradictory to what you desire.

Paul drew his confidence from the five doctrines cited in Romans 8:29-30: foreknowledge, predestination (or election), calling, justification, and glorification. In these words we have a description of God's sovereign, redemptive plan.

If you read carefully, you'll notice that Paul uses the past tense when listing each of these doctrines (e.g. "And those he predestined, he also called"). There's nothing tentative or speculative about these statements. Each aspect of God's redemptive plan is referred to as if it has already been accomplished in our lives. That's the eternal perspective, as Bible scholar F.F. Bruce has noted:

> The foreknowing and foreordaining belong to God's eternal counsel; the calling and justifying have taken place in his people's experience; but the glory, so far as their experience is concerned, lies in the future. Why then does Paul use the same past tense for this as he does for the other acts of God? Perhaps he is imitating the Hebrew use of the 'prophetic past,' by which a predicted event is marked out as so certain

---

2 Which of the following would be most likely to rattle your confidence in the care or character of God?

❑ Major financial problems

❑ Diagnosis of cancer

❑ Sudden death of a close friend or family member

❑ Sustained unemployment

❑ The thought of hell

❑ Other_____

❝ The conviction that Christian doctrine matters for Christian living is one of the most important growth points of the Christian life.[3] **❞**

— **Sinclair Ferguson**

of fulfillment that it is described as though it had already taken place. As a matter of history, the people of God have not yet been glorified. So far as divine decree is concerned, however, their glory has been determined from all eternity.[4]

Meditate on Hebrews 11:1. Do you assess your justification on the basis of personal emotion and experience or God's promise?

I had an experience a number of years ago that may help to clarify all this. As a native of the Washington, D.C. area and an avid sports fan, I was more than a little interested in the 1988 Superbowl match-up between the Washington Redskins and the Denver Broncos. I was also more than a little cynical about the Redskins' ability to perform under pressure—especially after watching Broncos quarterback John Elway throw an 80-yard touchdown on the first play. I spent the first quarter of the game in a certain degree of torment, my body contorting with each play as if my nervous, involuntary spasms would improve the Redskins' performance.

In the second quarter, however, the Redskins broke the game wide open as Doug Williams threw an unprecedented four touchdown passes. My cynicism slowly disappeared and the team went on to win convincingly.

What's interesting is the way I watched the game as it was unfolding and the way I later watched the videotape of the game. The second time around was much different. I was relaxed. I was enjoying the food. I *knew* the outcome before I even started watching. No matter how much Broncos fans celebrated Elway's quick touchdown, I knew that within minutes the domination would begin.

> **❝** His sovereignty can never be successfully challenged. He's in charge. It's scary, but it also brings a deep sense of security. We're cared for.[5] **❞**
>
> — James Cantelon

What's the point? God is as certain about the future as we are about the past. He wants to impart that certainty and security to us in the present. He wants us to *know* we have been justified, to *know* all things work together for good, to *know* nothing can separate us from Christ's love.

Do you know? Do you share Paul's certainty? Or do you still have doubts about the plan or providence of God?

God intends for us to embrace and enjoy his plan of redemption as an accomplished fact in our lives. Now it's true our glorification hasn't taken place yet—that won't happen until Jesus returns and we receive new bodies. But we are to live in the good of this plan that's being laid out for us, beginning in eternity past and extending into eterni-

Meditate on Isaiah 6:1-7. What prompted Isaiah to cry out, "Woe to me!" Have you ever seen yourself the way he did?

ty future. The impact on us in the present is that we can live both certain and secure that he who began a good work in us will bring it to completion until the day of Jesus Christ. When you understand foreknowledge (to the small degree that is possible), when you grasp election, when you appreciate call, when you benefit from justification, when you anticipate glorification, you realize that God is overwhelmingly, obviously *for* you. Nothing can separate you from the love of Jesus Christ! And even if your microwave nukes itself tomorrow or your car disappears, you can know that all things work together for the good because you love God and are called according to his purpose.

For the rest of our lives and throughout eternity we will be marveling at these aspects of God's character and plan. How undeserving we are of his foreknowledge, predestination, calling, justification, and glorification! Though everything will be more understandable once we're glorified with him, we will be no less in awe of our great salvation.

Let's not wait for the end of the age, though. Exploring our great salvation *now* will make a huge difference in the way we respond to accusation and adversity as we serve the purpose of God.

The Power of Theology

For Further Study: Authentic Christians will consistently draw flak and opposition from their society. Brace yourself by reading John 15:20-21 and 2 Timothy 3:12.

A crucial transition occurs in Romans 8:31. Paul asks, "What then shall we say in response to this?" As it turns out, Paul has plenty to say in the next nine verses. And once we have acquainted ourselves with foreknowledge, predestination, calling, justification, and glorification, we'll be able to respond to this great salvation with the intense conviction Paul exemplifies. Check this out.

God is for us (v.31). Could this be true? If you began this chapter unsure about God's predisposition, wonder no more. *He is for you.* He has convincingly demonstrated that, as we'll see in a few paragraphs. The basis for understanding whether or not God is for us is not subjective. Our emotional state is irrelevant. The objective, eternal fact of the matter is that God is for us.

Who can be against us (v.31)? This promise could easily be misinterpreted. Paul isn't saying that no one will ever be against you. In fact, both he and Jesus guaranteed just the opposite! However, no one who is against you will ever ultimately be successful because God is for you. No adversary can successfully challenge his sovereignty.

Consider the implications of this statement. Perhaps you are in a work situation where your boss appears to have something personal against you. Maybe he has even promoted others despite the fact that you were most qualified. That can be a very difficult test. So what do you do in that situation? You could begin looking for a new job, or go home and relieve your stress by watching tropical fish for a while. But there's a better way: Remind yourself that the sovereign God is for you. No matter what your employer does, Almighty God is for you and his purpose for your life will not be frustrated.

> **44** God sometimes allows people to treat us unjustly. Sometimes he even allows their actions to seriously affect our careers or our futures viewed on a human plane. But God never allows people to make decisions about us that undermine his plan for us. God is for us, we are his children, he delights in us (Zep 3:17)...We can put this down as a bedrock truth: God will never allow any action against you that is not in accord with his will for you. And his will is always directed to our good.[6] **77**
>
> — **Jerry Bridges**

If you can comprehend this, I guarantee that you will walk into your workplace tomorrow with a different attitude. Rather than resenting or resisting your employer, you'll be motivated to *serve* him or her! Such a dramatic transformation can only take place if you have grasped foreknowledge, predestination, calling, justification, and glorification. A right understanding of the doctrines of grace will forever change the way you view and respond to circumstances. Rather than taking revenge on your adversaries, you'll be able to love, pray for, and serve them.

Not even Satan can successfully oppose us. His power and authority tend to be overrated, anyway. We should be aware of him and maintain a certain degree of respect for his devices, but he is a created being. He cannot do anything without receiving permission from God. And listen—God is not indifferent to your situation. He has chosen you. He knows you by name. He is for you.

God gave his own Son for us (v.32). If you need proof that God is for you, look no further than the Cross. I cannot imagine what pain the Father must have experienced when he heard Jesus cry out, "My God, my God, why have you forsaken me?" He forsook his own Son so that we might know him as Father and never be forsaken ourselves. What further demonstration do we need? That bloody form hung there on the Cross to make this eternal proclamation: "I AM FOR YOU!"

For Further Study:
How should we respond to feelings and thoughts (including accusations) that contradict the promises of God's Word? (See 2 Corinthians 10:4-5)

3 Using an NIV translation of the Bible, fill in the missing blanks from Revelation 12:10:

"Now have come the _____ and

the _____ and the _____

of our God, and the authority of his

_____. For the _____ of

our brothers, who _____ them

before our God _____ and _____, has

been _____ _____."

**Meditate on
1 Corinthians 15:3.**
What significance did Paul attach to the crucifixion when presenting the gospel?

> ❝ Justification has eschatological implications. It means that the verdict which God will pronounce over us on the Day of Judgment has been brought into the present. We therefore do not need to fear the Judgment Day; we who believe in Christ have already crossed over from death to life.[7] ❞
>
> **— Anthony Hoekema**

No one can bring any charge against those God has chosen (v.33). You may be among those who know the torment of accusation. Past sins and failures relentlessly come to mind. No matter how many times you confess your sin, the memory of what you've done returns. But verse 33 is a legally binding statement: "Who will bring any charge against those whom God has chosen? It is God who justifies." The holy and just Judge of all has rendered a verdict that cannot be reversed. He has declared that because of the substitutionary sacrifice of his Son, you are now justified before him. Every time you hear accusations, affirm and declare that you have been justified by the finished work of Christ.

Who is he that condemns (v.34)? As liberating as it is to shake off demonic accusations, of ultimate importance is the fact that God himself will not condemn us. On that day when every knee bows before the judgment seat of Christ, countless multitudes will hear the horrific, irreversible words, "I never knew you. Depart from me, you who are cursed, into the eternal fire prepared for the devil and his angels." God doesn't *desire* to say this to anyone. He has put the Cross squarely in our path so that we can be spared these dreadful words. But those who have stubbornly gone around it, who have refused to submit to it, will be sentenced to eternal torment. Yet because you have received Christ's substitutionary sacrifice, no one can successfully bring a charge against you—not only in this lifetime but also at that critical moment when you stand before the judgment seat of God.

There's no more effective way to fight condemnation than to focus on the Cross. If you're lacking assurance or acceptance, fill your thoughts, your heart, and your worship with the Cross of Jesus Christ.

Jesus is interceding for us (v.34). In addition to the

wonder of his willing death on our behalf, our Lord prays for us from his authoritative position at the Father's right hand. He's not passively waiting for the end of the age, occasionally looking at his watch. Nor is he simply relaxing and receiving the sacrifice of our worship and service. He spends your entire lifetime interceding for you—by name.

Doesn't it encourage you to know Jesus himself is praying for your needs at this very moment?

Nothing shall separate us from the love of Christ (vv.35-39). When Paul says nothing, he means *nothing*. Trouble. Hardship. Persecution. Famine. Danger. Death. None of these can come between us and our Lord's love.

> For I am convinced that neither death nor life, neither angels nor demons, neither the present nor the future, nor any powers, neither height nor depth, nor anything else in all creation, will be able to separate us from the love of God that is in Christ Jesus our Lord (Ro 8:38-39).

When pounded by accusation or hounded by adversity, we can feel separated from God's love, as if he has abandoned us. An understanding of foreknowledge, predestination, calling, justification, and glorification delivers us from the unbiblical and unhelpful dependence on our fluctuating emotions at that time.

I know a man in England who could have reacted to his circumstances by charging God. I met Henry years ago at a conference. He is a respected Bible teacher and author in England and a man of proven character. In our interactions over the years I've been impressed with the kindness and care he consistently demonstrates.

During a recent visit to England I learned that Henry's wife had a serious illness and wasn't expected to live more than six months. I was surprised to see them present at the conference. Even more surprising was the joy so evident in their facial expressions. Almost unbelievable was

---

4 Write down the one problem or situation that's troubling you most right now.

Doesn't it encourage you to know that Jesus himself is praying for your needs at this very moment?

❝ Nothing in the expanses of space (nor height, nor depth) or in the course of time (nor things present, nor things to come), nothing in the whole universe of God (nor any other creature) can sever the children of God from their Father's love, secured to them in Christ.[8] ❞

— F.F. Bruce

Meditate on Philippians 1:21. How does this view of death compare with the world's view?

the way they were reaching out to other people. Instead of secluding themselves in self-pity, they were continuing to serve as normal. I was deeply affected.

Henry and I met at breakfast one morning during the conference. "C.J.," he said, "I'm sure you know what's happening with my wife. I've sought God, I've seen him heal many people, but I have no word that she'll be healed." I didn't know what to say. I was thinking to myself, *How can I respond? The next time I see him, his wife won't be with him.*

As it turned out I didn't need to say anything, because for the next 15 minutes Henry shared with me an invaluable lesson from Scripture and Church history on the subject of death. He quoted Charles Spurgeon, who described being most aware of God's glory when at the bedside of a dying saint. He also cited this statement made by John Wesley of an earlier generation: "Our people die well."

Henry's sorrow was evident. He made no attempt to conceal his grief. But he was convinced that death could not separate him or his wife from the love of Jesus Christ. Decades of studying and teaching the great truths of foreknowledge, predestination, calling, justification, and glorification had convinced them of God's sovereignty and love. They weren't afraid. They were secure. As Henry stood up and left I commented to a friend, "That's the power of understanding the doctrine of grace to change someone's life and sustain them in the midst of adversity."

> **“** How then does the Christian view death? He learns to see it in its proper perspective. He does not lightly and superficially dismiss it. Nor does he allow his life to be paralysed by the fear of it. He recognizes that death is an enemy, but he rejoices in the assurance that not even death can separate him from the love of Christ.[9] **”**
>
> **— Sinclair Ferguson**

At another point in the conference I was standing behind Henry as he worshiped. He turned back to me and said, "I'm going through my library and I have select books for certain men that I want to pass on to other generations. I'm going to be sending you a book." Not only was he prepared for his wife's death, but Henry was laboring to equip the next generation of leaders.

Don't feel sorry for him. I was the one all broken up inside. There he was, worshiping with a soft smile on his face. Why wasn't he bitter, depressed, complaining, or withdrawn? How could he minister joy to people in the midst of such deep, personal sorrow? Because Romans

8:38-39 was engraved on his heart: He knew that nothing could separate him from the love of Christ.

As the truths about this great salvation penetrate your heart, the result will be an ability to respond to accusation and adversity knowing and declaring that if God is for you no one can successfully oppose you, that he has justified you, and that nothing can separate you from his love.

If this book attempted to explore all five doctrines highlighted in this first chapter—foreknowledge, predestination, calling, justification, and glorification—it would be several hundred pages longer. (Actually, we would still be in the process of writing it!) We have opted to use the next six studies to focus on just one: the magnificent doctrine of justification by faith.

As you work through these pages, please don't be intimidated by the theology and doctrine you will cover. This stuff is full of life...and it will change your life. You will be awe-struck by the gift of justification that Jesus secured for us at the Cross. You will become convinced that God is for you, that all things are working together for good in your life, and that no one ultimately can oppose you with any degree of success. How overwhelming! And how totally undeserved. Truly this is amazing grace. ■

GROUP DISCUSSION

1. What's your single biggest fear?

2. An understanding of our great salvation is the perfect remedy for two common ailments. What are they? (Page 4)

3. Have you ever blamed God when something went wrong?

4. How do you handle anxiety and stress?

5. Is there any area where Satan consistently accuses you?

6. Glance back at the Superbowl story on page 5. How does this affect your understanding of Romans 8:29-30?

7. How did you respond to Question #4 on page 9?

8. It's too easy to keep theology locked up in our brains rather than letting it influence our behavior. What effect will this chapter have on your daily life?

RECOMMENDED READING

God's Words: Studies of Key Bible Themes by J.I. Packer (Grand Rapids, MI: Baker Book House, 1981)

The Pilgrim's Progress by John Bunyan (various editions available, including an inexpensive Penguin Classic)

Romans by John Stott (Downers Grove, IL: InterVarsity Press, 1995)

Still Sovereign by Thomas R. Schreiner and Bruce A. Ware, eds. (Grand Rapids, MI: Baker Book House, 2000)

CHAPTER TWO

DOES ANYONE BELIEVE IN SIN?

ROBIN BOISVERT

O ne Saturday afternoon some years ago I was hard at work cleaning out the garage. My oldest son, then about four, was on hand to help...so to speak. I watched him as he eyed various dangerous items.

"What's this, Dad?"

"That's Daddy's wood chisel. Don't touch it."

"What's this, Dad?"

"That's the gasoline can. Stay away from it, please. Hey! Don't pick up that saw, son."

Things went on like that for a while until, finally exasperated, my son blurted out, "Daddy! Everything you tell me not to do is just what I *want* to do!"

Probably just what Adam said, I thought to myself. I could now rest secure in the knowledge that my son was an authentic member of the human race. And so it is with all of us.

What's the Problem?

Take an informal poll of neighbors, friends, and co-workers and ask them what they consider to be mankind's most basic problem. The answer would likely be ignorance or a lack of education. "If people were just better - educated, if they could see the bigger picture, then there wouldn't be all the difficulties," they might tell you. "More sex education would prevent AIDS and unwanted pregnancies. More education could eliminate racism and the misunderstandings that separate people. Better education would enable the poor to get better jobs and avoid drugs and crime."

Thomas Greer, in a recent Western Civilization textbook, states that during the eighteenth-century Enlightenment period, science and education were considered by

**Meditate on Romans
1:22.** What is God's
one-word assessment
of man's "enlightened"
ideas?

important thinkers to be the answers to the human
dilemma. Says Greer, "The world would never be quite the
same again; the belief in science and education became a
feature of the modern world. In the United States, found-
ed at the peak of the Enlightenment, *that belief has
remained an article of national faith though it is being
questioned today more than ever*" (emphasis added).[1]
While it's certainly true that ignorance claims its share of
victims, there is a problem yet more basic.

One of those questioning that "article of national faith"
was the eminent psychiatrist Karl Menninger. In the early
1970s he wrote a small book with the provocative title,
"Whatever Became of Sin?" In it he observed that the
word "sin" and the concept it represented began to disap-
pear from our culture around the middle of the twentieth
century.

> In all of the laments and reproaches made by our
> seers and prophets, one misses any mention of 'sin,'
> a word which used to be a veritable watchword of
> prophets. It was a word once in everyone's mind,
> but now rarely if ever heard. Does that mean that no
> sin is involved in all our troubles—sin with an 'I' in
> the middle? Is no one any longer guilty of anything?
> Guilty perhaps of a sin that could be repented or
> repaired or atoned for? Is it only that someone may
> be stupid or sick or criminal— or asleep? Wrong
> things are being done, we know; tares are being
> sown in the wheat field at night. But is no one
> responsible; is no one answerable for these acts?
> Anxiety and depression we all acknowledge, and
> even vague guilt feelings; but has no one committed
> any sins?…The very word 'sin,' which seems to have
> disappeared, was a proud word. It was once a strong
> word, an ominous and serious word. It described a
> central point in every civilized human being's life
> plan and life style. But the word went away. It has
> almost disappeared—the word, along with the
> notion. Why? Doesn't anyone sin anymore? Doesn't
> anyone believe in sin?[2]

Dr. Menninger should be applauded for going much
further than others in his field. And he is surely correct in
his observations as far as they go. A moral model of
understanding human responsibilities and problems has
been all but replaced by a medical model, so that individuals who commit heinous crimes are rarely referred to as

"wicked" or "evil" or "sinful," but as "sick" or "mentally ill" or "insane." A closer examination of Dr. Menninger's book, however, shows that despite his appeal for society to reconsider sin as a means for understanding human nature, he himself has a grossly inadequate grasp of the issue. He views sin on an entirely horizontal level, the sin of one person against another or perhaps against oneself. To fully comprehend the nature of sin, though, we must recognize its vertical dimension: sin is primarily an *offense toward God*.

Psalm 51 provides us with a vivid example of this truth. In this psalm David pours out his heart to God in repentance. He had been outwardly rebuked by the prophet Nathan and inwardly convicted by the Spirit for his adultery with Bathsheba and for arranging the death of her husband as a cover-up. Yet in spite of what he had done, David cries to God, "Against you, you only have I sinned and done what is evil in your sight" (Ps 51:4). David was not denying his sin against Bathsheba and Uriah, but he was acknowledging the ugliest characteristic of any sin, regardless of its type: it is against God.

For Further Study:
What three things does an inaccurate view of sin reveal about us? (See 1 John 1:8-10)

Sin—what an *unpleasant* subject! And a difficult one, besides. But it is absolutely essential that we consider this matter, because if our perception of sin is incorrect, so will be our knowledge of God, Jesus Christ, the Holy Spirit, the law of God, the gospel, and the way of salvation. An accurate understanding of sin is the bottom button on the shirt of Christian theology. If it's out of place, the whole garment will be hopelessly askew.

The Seriousness of Sin

Minimizing sin is as common as sin itself. It's not unusual to hear people refer to their own sin as a "weakness" or "shortcoming." "Nobody's perfect," they say. They may even be courageous enough to admit, "I made an error in judgment." But sin is no minor issue. If there is no sin, then there is no salvation. If we are not great sinners, then Christ is no great Savior.

The fact that we're all affected by sin puts us at a disad-

> **"** Sin is the dare of God's justice, the rape of his mercy, the jeer of his patience, the slight of his power and the contempt of his love.[4] **"**
>
> — **John Bunyan**

vantage in our attempt to understand it. On our own, we simply cannot come to clear views on the matter. Thankfully, God has provided us with his infallible Word on the subject. The beginning chapters of Genesis spell out humanity's sinful dilemma, and the remainder of Scripture can be read as God's solution to the problem.

Within the space of five short verses the Bible describes us as helpless, ungodly, sinners, and enemies of God (Ro 5:6-10). God's Word tells us that sin is universal. Sin is deceitful. Sin is also tenacious and powerful. Sin is so overwhelming that only one force in the universe can overcome it. Only one force, resident in one Person, can overcome it because only one Person has ever been without it. As the angel told Mary, "You are to give him the name Jesus, because he will save his people from their sins" (Mt 1:21).

Meditate on John 1:29. What's the significance of the title John the Baptist gives Jesus? (See Exodus 12:21-23)

Complementing the teaching of Scripture are the testimonies of godly men and women throughout the Church's history who have been aware of their sinfulness in direct proportion to their nearness to God. Just listen to how these great saints of the Bible evaluated themselves:

David: "I have sinned against the Lord" (2Sa 12:13).

Isaiah: "I am a man of unclean lips" (Isa 6:5).

Peter: "Go away from me, Lord; I am a sinful man!" (Lk 5:8)

Paul: "Christ Jesus came into the world to save sinners—of whom I am the worst" (1Ti 1:15).

1 Paul's claim to be the worst of sinners must have been challenged many, many times since he wrote those words. What evidence could you present from the last 24 hours to argue that you are actually history's worst sinner? (Think about it just long enough to genuinely repent, then go on.)

Sin is the transgression of the law (1Jn 3:4). God gave the law and stands behind it. When we break God's laws, he takes it personally. If we could see God standing behind every situation where his law is broken and feel his righteous anger, we would better comprehend the seriousness of sin.

For Further Study: Note the atrocities committed by Eli's sons (1 Samuel 2:12-25) and God's response (1 Samuel 2:27-34).

The Israelite priest Eli reproved his foolish and immoral sons with these words: "If a man sins against another man, God may mediate for him; but if a man sins against the Lord, who will intercede for him?" (1Sa 2:25). Unfortunately, his words were too little and too late to turn his sons around. They were not sufficiently aware of the seriousness of sin.

16

Welcome to the Pig Pen

The essence of sin has been described as self-centeredness. This thought is captured well in Isaiah 53:6: "We all, like sheep, have gone astray, each of us has turned to his own way." Let's take a closer look at the implications of this verse.

Like sheep. Among the least intelligent of all barnyard animals, sheep are usually unaware of danger until it's too late.

Gone astray. The natural tendency of sheep is to wander. Unless the shepherd keeps them in the flock, they quickly get off track.

For Further Study: Broaden your understanding of sin's seriousness by reading Romans 8:6-7, Colossians 1:21, and Ephesians 2:1-2.

Each of us. Sin is a universal problem, affecting us all.

His own way. This is the heart of the matter. We want to live our lives without reference to the God who made us and sustains us, and to whom we are indebted for our next breath. Hear these words by William Ernest Henley, a "stray sheep" who seems to have been hardened in his own way:

> It matters not how strait the gate,
> How charged with punishment the scroll;
> I am the master of my fate,
> I am the captain of my soul.[5]

The scope of sin is so great that the Bible uses many words to convey its appalling nature and disastrous effects. Wrapped up in that one little word are ideas such as rebellion, wickedness, confusion, shame, missing the mark, unfaithfulness, lawlessness, ignorance, disobedience, perversion, and more.

Anyone reading the first three chapters of Paul's letter to the Roman Christians is struck by his scathing indictment of the human race. Both Jew and Gentile are locked up in the bondage of sin. Paul's words are so forceful and unequivocal that the reader's tendency is to regard Paul's reasoning as extreme. "Hey, he must be talking about Jack the Ripper or Adolf Hitler!" But he's not. He's talking about you and me. "There is no one righteous, not even one... There is no one who does good...all have sinned and fall short of the glory of God" (Ro 3:10, 12, 23). This paints an extremely uncomplimentary portrait of the human race.

Part of our problem is that we tend to evaluate our sinfulness in relation to other people. Compared to Attila the Hun, I'm doing swell. But compared to Mother Teresa, I'm not. Unless God reveals the extent of our sin to us, we cannot discern our own depravity.

During the 1980s I lived in the beautiful farm country of Lancaster, Pennsylvania. Life there was pleasant in all respects but one: I never got used to the smell of manure. Pigs were by far the worst. But interestingly, though I found their odor disgusting, the pigs didn't seem to mind in the least. As J.C. Ryle has put it, "The very animals whose smell is most offensive to us have no idea they are offensive and are not offensive to one another."[7] Fallen man, it seems, can have no adequate idea what a vile thing sin is in the sight of a holy and perfect God.

> " He that hath slight thoughts of sin, never had great thoughts of God.[6] "
> — John Owen

How did we fall into this sad state of affairs?

What ever happened to the human race?

Can a Leopard Change Its Spots?

In the fifth chapter of Romans (verses 12-21), Paul explains both the source of our sin and the source of our ultimate forgiveness. It should be noted at the outset that our discussion of man's sinfulness relates to his natural state apart from grace. Through Christ's redemptive work, man's relationship to sin has been radically changed.

Sin came upon all men because of the sin of one man—Adam. This is proven by the fact that all men die, physical death being the penalty for sin.

When I was a junior in high school, we studied the Puritan era in America. I recall seeing an illustration of a reading primer containing the following: "In Adam's fall, we sinned all." I can still remember how provoked I was by those words. At the time I thought, *It's just wrong to brainwash children like that!* Then, thinking more in terms of myself, I really got upset. *I don't see why I should be dragged down with Adam. After all, I don't know him from Adam!* To say I found this doctrine offensive would be an understatement. It offends our sense of fairness. The natural man finds it extremely objectionable. (Which is one of the main reasons I now believe it's true.)

Paul's point in describing our inherent sinfulness is not to irritate but to inform. Understanding our relationship to Adam gives us a fresh appreciation for our relationship with Jesus Christ. Renowned pastor D. Martyn Lloyd-Jones has written, "If you say to me, 'Is it fair that the sin of Adam should be imputed (charged) to me?' I will reply by asking, 'Is it fair that the righteousness of Christ should be imputed to you?'"[9]

Sin is the universal inheritance handed down from our common father, Adam. We are by nature guilty and antagonistic toward God. This teaching is known as original sin and it describes man's fallen condition. It directly contradicts the idea that we all enter the world with a clean slate, sinless and innocent. Although man continues to bear the image and likeness of God, that image has been defaced. He is now like the ruins of an ancient temple. The marks of grandeur are still evident, but the glory has departed. As with a cracked mirror, the image remains but is largely distorted.

Original sin involves two further aspects:

Total depravity. This is a term generally misunderstood and therefore discounted. It does not mean that man is as bad as he could possibly be. That would be *utter* depravity. Total depravity indicates that sin's corruption affects man in every part of his being: his mind, his emotions, his will, and his body. There is nothing in man that has not been affected by sin.

Total inability. This does not mean that man cannot do anything good by *human* standards. He can still perform outward acts of righteousness and may possess many fine qualities. But in

HOW WE GOT INTO THE PIT

Suppose God said to a man, "I want you to trim these bushes by three o'clock this afternoon. But be careful. There is a large open pit at the edge of the garden. If you fall into that pit, you will not be able to get yourself out. So whatever you do, stay away from that pit."

Suppose that as soon as God leaves the garden the man runs over and jumps into the pit. At three o'clock God returns and finds the bushes untrimmed. He calls for the gardener and hears a faint cry from the edge of the garden. He walks to the edge of the pit and sees the gardener helplessly flailing around on the bottom. He says to the gardener, "Why haven't you trimmed the bushes I told you to trim?" The gardener responds in anger, "How do you expect me to trim these bushes when I am trapped in this pit? If you hadn't left this empty pit here, I would not be in this predicament."

Adam jumped into the pit. In Adam we all jumped into the pit. God did not throw us into the pit. Adam was clearly warned about the pit. God told him to stay away. The consequences Adam experienced from being in the pit were a direct punishment for jumping into it...

We are born sinners because in Adam all fell. Even the word "fall" is a bit of a euphemism. It is a rose-colored view of the matter. The word "fall" suggests an accident of sorts. Adam's sin was not an accident. He was not Humpty-Dumpty. Adam didn't simply slip into sin; he jumped into it with both feet. We jumped headlong with him.[8]

— R.C. Sproul

regard to *spiritual* things, he is powerless. Even the "good" things he does are tainted by sin. To paraphrase the Westminster Confession on the subject, "having fallen into sin, man has completely lost his ability to do anything to contribute to his salvation."

Donald MacLeod says, "[Total inability] means that conversion is beyond the capacity of the natural man."[10] Apart from Christ, nothing that a man does can please God because he is neither motivated by God's grace nor concerned for God's glory. And God is supremely concerned with our motives.

Jeremiah gives expression to total inability when he asks, "Can the Ethiopian change his skin or the leopard its spots? Neither can you do good who are accustomed to doing evil" (Jer 13:23). When Paul told the Ephesians that they had been *dead* in trespasses and sins, he was helping them understand not only the overwhelming grace of God in saving them, but their absolute need for that grace. A dead person can in no way participate in his salvation.

So what happens after conversion? Is sin no longer present? Oh, if that were only the case! Sin's power over one who has been born again is certainly broken. Romans 6 clarifies that while the presence of sin is still a factor, our connection with it has been radically altered. The Holy Spirit now dwells within us, showing us the way to walk in God. We are no longer enslaved to sin. It doesn't dominate or master us; we're not obligated to obey sin's promptings. The threat of judgment no longer hangs over our heads. Yet we continue to feel sin's influence.

One helpful way of understanding our deliverance from sin employs three different verb tenses: We *have*

---

2 Which of the following suggest that even children are tainted by original sin?

❏ The ease with which they learn to say "No!"

❏ The ease with which they can forget to do what they're told.

❏ The amazing way that two children can to want the same toy—the one they haven't cared about for six weeks—at the same time, ignoring all other available toys.

❏ The universality of tantrums and sulking.

For Further Study:
What role does water baptism play in our struggle against sin? (See Ro 6:1-11)

❝ He who looks upon sin merely as a fiction, as a misfortune, or as a trifle, sees no necessity either for deep repentance or a great atonement. He who sees no sin in himself will feel no need of a Saviour. He who is conscious of no evil at work in his heart, will desire no change of nature. He who regards sin as a slight affair will think a few tears or an outward reformation ample satisfaction. The truth is no man ever thought himself a greater sinner before God than he really was. Nor was any man ever more distressed at his sin than he had just cause to be.[11] ❞

— **William S. Plumer**

been delivered from the **penalty** of sin; we *are being* delivered from the **power** of sin; we *shall be* delivered from the **presence** of sin. Nevertheless, as ironic as it sounds, the closer one walks with God, the greater will be his knowledge and awareness of sin. I recall as a child being fascinated by dust particles dancing about in a ray of light beaming through the window. The dust was everywhere present, but was only made visible by the light. So also with sin. It is made manifest by the light of God's Word and Spirit. The stronger the light, the more evident the dust.

3 What one or two words would you associate with the penalty of sin? The power of sin? The presence of sin? Write those under the appropriate headings below.

Penalty   **Power**   **Presence**

Ugly Weeds with Deep Roots

As a lover of old books, especially the writings of the Puritans, I have often found myself struggling with the emphasis earlier generations put on sin, even in the lives of the converted. *Where was the victory in their lives?* I wondered during my initial encounters with their writings. I've since come to understand that their awareness of sin, as acute as it was, did not exceed their awareness of the grace and mercy of God in forgiveness of that sin.

Consider Jonathan Edwards, for example, known as much for his holy life as for his great learning. Edwards referred to having a "vastly greater sense of my own wickedness and the badness of my heart than ever I had before my conversion"—a sign of spiritual health, in his opinion![12] His descendant and biographer, Serano Dwight, felt the need to explain his grandfather's thinking. It wasn't that Edwards *had* more wickedness, wrote Dwight, but that he had a greater *sense* of it. He then clarified his observation with an analogy:

> Suppose a blind man had a garden full of ugly and poisonous weeds. They are present in his garden but he is not aware of them. Now suppose that garden is, for the most part, cleared of the weeds, and many beautiful and worthwhile plants and flowers have replaced them. The man then regains his sight. There are *fewer* weeds, but he is more aware of them. So, the clearer our spiritual vision, the greater our awareness of sin.[13]

The following words by J.C. Ryle provide an eloquent conclusion for our chapter on the doctrine of sin:

Meditate on Romans 5:20-21. How does an awareness of sin deepen our gratitude for the grace of God?

Sin—this infection of nature does remain, yes even in them that are regenerate. So deeply planted are the roots of human corruption, that even after we are born again, renewed, washed, sanctified, justified, and made living members of Christ, these roots remain alive in the bottom of our hearts and, like the leprosy in the walls of the house, we never get rid of them until the earthly house of this tabernacle is dissolved. Sin, no doubt, in the believer's heart, no longer has dominion. It is checked, controlled, mortified, and crucified by the expulsive power of the new principle of grace. The life of a believer is a life of victory and not of failure. But the very struggles that go on within him, the fight that he finds it needful to fight daily, the watchful jealousy he is obliged to exercise over his inner man, the contest between the flesh and the spirit, the inward groanings *which no one knows but he who has experienced them*—all testify to the same great truth: the enormous power and vitality of sin…. Happy is the believer who understands it and, while he rejoices in Christ Jesus, has no confidence in the flesh, and while he says thanks be to God who gives us the victory, never forgets to watch and pray lest he fall into temptation."[15] ∎

> " I have no tolerance for those who exalt psychology above Scripture, intercession, and the perfect sufficiency of our God. And I have no encouragement for people who wish to mix psychology with the divine resources and sell the mixture as a spiritual elixir. Their methodology amounts to a tacit admission that what God has given us in Christ is not really adequate to meet our deepest needs and salve our troubled lives.[14] "
>
> — **John MacArthur, Jr.**

GROUP DISCUSSION

1. Split the group into two teams, the "Science/ Education" side and the "Salvation" side. Let each team alternate in proposing social ills it could cure. Which team did the most good for humanity?

2. "A moral model of understanding human responsibilities and problems has been all but replaced by a medical model," says the author (Page 14). What evidence of that shift do you see in the body of Christ?

3. Isn't God mature enough not to be bothered by our insignificant little sins?

4. On a scale of one to ten, rate what your lifestyle says about the seriousness of sin. (1 = not at all serious, 10 = very serious)

5. How is the essence of sin defined? (Page 17) Do you agree?

6. Read Romans 3:10-18 aloud. Be totally honest: Do you struggle with the fact that this describes *you* apart from God's redeeming grace?

7. What did we inherit from Adam? From Jesus?

8. How would you explain "total inability" (Pages 19-20) to a non-Christian?

9. Review the three tenses of our deliverance from sin (Pages 20-21). How did this explanation strike you?

10. Discuss the final sentence in the concluding quotation by J.C. Ryle (Page 22).

RECOMMENDED READING   *Chosen by God* by R.C. Sproul (Wheaton, IL: Tyndale House Publishers, 1986)

CHAPTER THREE

THE HOLINESS OF GOD

ROBIN BOISVERT

I was feeling pretty exuberant as I entered the meeting that night. When a good friend appeared, I shouted to him across the room, "Come on over here, in the name of Jesus!" Moments later another young man quietly drew me aside and expressed his concern that I was treating the name of Jesus in a flippant manner. Flushing red with embarrassment, I mumbled, "Thanks for pointing that out." It was apparent that he was concerned for me personally. I also knew he was right, and that he was showing more regard for God's honor than I had. Though I certainly didn't intend any harm, I realized from this incident that I had become overly familiar with the Lord's name.

It hadn't started out that way. At the time of my conversion three years before, I had been overwhelmed by God's power to change my life. Meetings pervaded by his presence and remarkable answers to prayer had convinced me of the reality of the Holy Spirit and the love of Jesus Christ. Who else could have so thoroughly overcome the depression and hopelessness that had engulfed me? But as the intensity of those first months gradually subsided into a more consistent faith, something else had crept in. God's majestic greatness was being eroded by a growing familiarity. It was high time to consider again the holiness of God.

Holiness. The word itself conjures up images of humorless monks in colorless monasteries eating tasteless food and leading joyless lives. Or perhaps long faces, long dresses, and long lists of "don'ts." But how about *beauty*? Does the word holiness prompt thoughts of beauty? Probably not. Yet beauty is a quality often associated with God's holiness. In the Psalms we're exhorted to worship the Lord "in the beauty of holiness" (Ps 29:2; 96:9 AV). Holiness is said to forever enhance the appearance of God's temple: "Your statutes stand firm; holiness adorns your house for endless days, O Lord" (Ps 93:5).

Meditate on 1 Chronicles 16:23-36. Do you pick up any sense of spiritual drudgery in David's attitude toward the holiness of God?

In spite of the clear and positive regard the Bible has for holiness, most of us would still equate it with drudgery. At the mere mention of the word our minds move toward what we perceive to be our responsibilities as Christians. But any accurate understanding of holiness must trace its way back to the source of all holiness—God himself. And when we view the holiness of God, we're not dealing with human responsibility at all but with God's most attractive and awe-inspiring attribute.

Theologian Stephen Charnock points out that among the various qualities of God, there are some we prefer because of the blessing we immediately gain from them. For instance, we would rather sing of the mercy of the Lord than think about his justice and wrath. We're more inclined to reflect on a loving Savior than to consider a jealous God. There are some divine attributes, however, that God himself delights in because they so perfectly express his excellence. Holiness is such an attribute.[1] Those mysterious heavenly beings, the seraphs and the four living creatures, know that the holiness of God must be underscored. Think of it. They dwell in his presence and have an unobstructed view of reality (while we see through a glass dimly). If any beings were ever "in the know," they are. And so, over and over, day and night, they never cease crying out, "Holy, holy, holy is the Lord God Almighty" (Is 6:3, Rev 4:8).

Holiness differs from God's other perfections in that it spreads itself throughout all the other attributes. Thus his love is a *holy* love, his justice a *holy* justice, and so forth. If God's attributes could be thought of as the various facets of a diamond, then holiness would be the combined brightness of those facets shining out in radiant glory.

Religious Superstitions

Meditate on Matthew 5:17-20. Do you think this could explain why the New Testament contains about 90 references to the book of Leviticus?

Scripture has a great deal to say about holiness. The first book of the Bible, Genesis, outlines man's ruin. Then Exodus, with its central image of the Passover lamb, shows his recovery. Next comes the book of Leviticus. Ah, Leviticus—that book in which so many aspiring students of the Bible have bogged down in their annual attempt to read through the Bible, never to reappear. Yet this book is crucial to our understanding of holiness. Leviticus also sheds important light on the sacrificial atonement of our Lord Jesus Christ.

In the book of Leviticus God shows man how to

approach him in worship. The book focuses primarily on the different sacrifices that God required in order for his people to *get right* with him, and then the different feasts God ordained so that they could *stay right* with him.[2] As confusing and irrelevant as this elaborate sacrificial system may appear to us today, God instituted it in order to instruct his people in the profound truth that *he is holy*.

> ❝ It is always necessary to remind ourselves of the grandeur of this absolute moral perfection, which encircles the Divine Person. Without it, true worship would degenerate and man would become presumptuous.[3] ❞
>
> — **T.C. Hammond**

The word holiness implies a separation from all that is impure.[4] God is different from us. He is *other* than we are. Though this may seem elementary, it needs to be stated because of current notions about "New Age" powers within us and a supposed inherent divinity of mankind.

In Scripture, the ordinary things that God touches become extraordinary. For example, because it was the place of divine revelation, the area surrounding the burning bush was marked out as holy ground and it became appropriate for Moses to remove his sandals out of reverence for God. Or consider the utensils used in the service of the tabernacle and the temple. They weren't ordinary either. They were holy. So also were holy assemblies, holy altars, holy anointing oil, and holy days.

What made them holy? A holy God. God selected common things and made them special by setting them apart for holy purposes, specifically to communicate to his people that *he* is holy.

Unfortunately, many people miss this point badly and end up in religious superstition. I once received a late-night call from an elderly lady requesting that I meet her for prayer. She insisted that it couldn't wait and that we must meet at "the house of God." I suggested that, considering the hour, a public place might be more appropriate than an empty church building, but she kept insisting that we meet at "the house of God." This dear lady had fallen into the error of ascribing to a place a certain special quality that belongs to God alone. She did not realize that in this New Testament era, no place is inherently holy—not even the "Holy Land."

The prophet Jeremiah, aware of a similar attitude among his people, wrote, "Do not trust in deceptive words and say, 'This is the temple of the Lord, the temple of the Lord, the temple of the Lord!'" (Jer 7:4). Despite their rev-

For Further Study:
The Pharisees carried religious superstition to the extreme, as seen in Matthew 23:16-22. Did Jesus commend their behavior?

1 The Bible passages below demonstrate three cases where reverence for a religious artifact, ritual, or building damaged the people's relationship with God. In the space below each reference, briefly summarize the problem.

■ Numbers 21:6-9; 2 Kings 18:1-4

■ Luke 13:10-16

■ Mark 13:1-2; Matthew 26:59-62; Matthew 12:3-6

Meditate on 1 Samuel 6:19-20. Does your awe of God match that the men of Beth Shemesh experienced?

erence for the temple's physical structure, the Israelites who kept repeating "The temple of the Lord" regrettably had hearts far removed from the Lord of the temple.

I see the same thing happen when unsaved couples who have no interest in following Jesus Christ nevertheless consider it absolutely essential that they be married in a church building. What else can this be but a superstitious feeling that somehow their marriage will be blessed if it takes place in a "holy" building? Putting undue emphasis on buildings or ceremonies or religious artifacts does nothing to show honor and respect for God.

God, in Scripture, did set apart certain things for special use, but he had a point in doing so—to teach us that *he* is holy and must be held in respect. For this reason, then, to use holy things in a profane or common manner was offensive to God.

The fifth chapter of Daniel recounts the familiar story of the handwriting on the wall, when God inscribed his divine judgment against the king of Babylon. What prompted his wrath? Belshazzar had profaned what God declared holy, as Daniel recounts: "So they brought in the gold goblets that had been taken from the temple of God in Jerusalem, and the king and his nobles, his wives and his concubines drank from them. As they drank the wine, they praised the gods of gold and silver, of bronze, iron, wood and stone" (Da 5:3-4).

When Daniel was called in to decipher the mysterious writing, he took the opportunity to roundly rebuke the king. His final words summed up Belshazzar's sin: "You did not honor the God who holds in his hand your life and all your ways" (Da 5:23).

Belshazzar's failure to honor the things of God amounted to a failure to honor God; his blasphemy cost him his life. Incidents like this are sprinkled throughout the Bible to warn of what can happen when someone decides to play fast and loose with the things of God. Whether immediately or at the end of the age, judgment will be enacted for sins against God's holiness.

The "Disintegration Factor"

God is so different from us. Though we're created in his image, his thoughts and his ways are so far beyond ours that Isaiah likens it to the distance between the heavens and the earth (Isa. 55: 8, 9). Perhaps this is nowhere clearer than in regard to his moral excellence. As the prophet Habakkuk expressed it, "Your eyes are too pure to look on evil; you cannot tolerate wrong" (Hab 1:13).

God's absolute purity goes beyond mere sinlessness. It is a positive expression of his goodness, not just the absence of sin. We've all met people whose character shines so much brighter than our own that we feel small and stained by comparison. I have a friend who, before he shaved off his beard, looked like a combination of Abraham Lincoln and Jesus (as depicted in contemporary illustrations, that is). The similarity isn't merely in physical appearance, either. His kindness and gentle wisdom are truly exceptional. Though it would distress him to know this, being around him reminds me of my own selfishness. If human comparisons can make us feel that low, imagine the discomfort we would feel in the presence of a holy God!

> **"** How slow we are to believe in God as *God*, sovereign, all-seeing and almighty! How little we make of the majesty of our Lord and Saviour Jesus Christ! The need for us is to 'wait upon the Lord' in meditations of his majesty, till we find our strength renewed through the writing of these things upon our hearts.[5] **"**
>
> — **J.I. Packer**

This is exactly what happened to Peter. Jesus amazed Peter one day by providing a miraculous catch of fish. But instead of rejoicing in the haul, all Peter could see was his own sinfulness. When confronted with the holiness of Jesus, Peter saw himself as he really was, and the reality of it was devastating. "Simon Peter...fell at Jesus' knees and said, 'Go away from me, Lord; I am a sinful man!'" (Lk 5:8).

It didn't take Peter long to lose sight of the Lord's holiness, as we see four chapters later on the mount of transfiguration. This sublime incident featured a visit from two of the most celebrated persons of Israel's past, Moses and Elijah. To top it off, a transfigured Jesus became as bright as lightning. Yet Peter, instead of falling before the Lord as he had done previously, seemed oblivious to what was taking place. He became chatty and suggested that maybe they could make some temporary shelters for everyone. That's when God the Father intervened personally. "While [Peter] was speaking, a cloud appeared and enveloped

For Further Study:
If you want fresh revelation of God's sovereign power and holiness, try this abbreviated word study of "tremble"— Exodus 15:13-16; Job 9:4-6; Psalms 99:1-3; Isaiah 64:1-4; Jeremiah 23:9; Ezekiel 38:20-23; Joel 3:16; Habakkuk 3:6.

2 Read John's description of Jesus Christ in Revelation 1:10-16. What details strike you most vividly?

them, and they were afraid as they entered the cloud. A voice came from the cloud, saying, 'This is my Son, whom I have chosen; listen to him'" (Lk 9:34-35). This seems to have had a sobering effect on Peter and the others, for as Matthew points out, "When the disciples heard this, they fell face down to the ground, terrified" (Mt 17:6).

The prophet Isaiah had a dramatic experience which marked him forever. He saw a vision of the Lord "seated on a throne, high and exalted, and the train of his robe filled the temple" (Is 6:1). In this vision angelic beings were declaring the overwhelming holiness of God. "At the sound of their voices the doorposts and thresholds shook and the temple was filled with smoke" (v.4). Utterly undone by the awesome display, Isaiah responded in the only appropriate way: "Woe to me! I am ruined! For I am a man of unclean lips, and I live among a people of unclean lips, and my eyes have seen the King, the Lord Almighty" (v.5).

> ❝ When [God's] divine judgment fell on Nadab or Uzzah, the response was shock and outrage. We have come to expect God to be merciful. From there the next step is easy: we demand it. When it is not forthcoming, our first response is anger against God, coupled with the protest: "It isn't fair." We soon forget that with our first sin we have forfeited all rights to the gift of life. That I am drawing breath this morning is an act of divine mercy. God owes me nothing. I owe him everything.[6] ❞
>
> **— R.C. Sproul**

Some have called Isaiah's experience the "disintegration factor." R.C. Sproul writes, "For the first time in his life Isaiah really understood who God was. At the same instant, for the first time Isaiah really understood who Isaiah was."[7] If the word "integrity" means wholeness (an integer is a whole number), disintegration means to be broken into pieces. Most of us are trying so hard to get our lives "together." And even if we're falling apart, we'd at least like to appear to be "together." How distressing, then, to be in the presence of God and fall completely apart as we discover the depth of our own sinfulness.

For Further Study:
The following passages reveal angelic encounters—Numbers 22:21-31; Judges 6:20-23; Matthew 28:2-4; Luke 2:8-10.

Approaching a Holy God

The awareness of one's sinfulness initially produces an aversion to God. In almost every biblical account of angelic visitations, the individuals fall down in abject fear. How much more those who see God in his awesome holiness? The Israelites who stood before Mount Sinai as it quaked with the holy presence of God begged Moses to be their intermediary, their go-between. Moses reminds them of this:

When you heard the voice out of the darkness, while the mountain was ablaze with fire, all the leading men of your tribes and your elders came to me. And you said, "The Lord our God has shown us his glory and his majesty, and we have heard his voice from the fire. Today we have seen that a man can live even if God speaks with him. But now, why should we die? This great fire will consume us, and we will die if we hear the voice of the Lord our God any longer. For what mortal man has ever heard the voice of the living God speaking out of fire, as we have, and survived? Go near and listen to all that the Lord our God says. Then tell us whatever the Lord our God tells you. We will listen and obey" (Dt 5:23-27).

I once heard John Wimber refer to people who do not want a relationship with God because they consider it too dangerous. They would prefer a relationship with Christianity or with the church. While this is undoubtedly the case with some, a true Christian has the desire to be holy. He knows that only the pure in heart shall see God (Mt 5:8), and he longs for that purity that will enable him to behold his Lord. For the maturing Christian, an awareness of God's holiness reassures him of God's love. He realizes that in spite of God's holiness and his own sinfulness, the Lord is long-suffering toward him. He deserves judgment but instead receives mercies which are new every morning.

3 In The Chronicles of Narnia, author C.S. Lewis uses the noble lion Aslan to portray Jesus. At one point a character says of Aslan, "It's not as if he were a tame lion."[9] Can you think of any examples from the Bible or your own interaction with God that show he isn't "tame"?

We may consider our attempts to live the Christian life to be feeble indeed, but if we have a desire for holiness we can take heart. God is the One who put that desire there and he is certain to bring it to pass. But how? How will we fulfill God's seemingly impossible command, "Be holy, because I am holy" (1Pe 1:16)? How can we approach "the blessed and only Ruler, the King of kings and Lord of lords, who alone is immortal and *who lives in unapproachable light,* whom no one has seen or can see" (1Ti 6:15-16, emphasis added)?

We must approach with reverence, as is strikingly displayed through the ministry of the Old Testament priest. In order for the priest to approach God, there were closely prescribed regulations. One could not go into the Holy of Holies anytime he wished. The high priest entered the most holy place just one day each year on the Day of Atonement. He first had to offer a sacrifice for himself, the blood serving as a reminder to him of his sinfulness and God's holiness. Then he had to dress in special garments. On the hem of his robe were alternating pomegranates and bells which would jingle to give evidence that he was still alive, that he had not been slain by the holiness of God. According to tradition, a length of rope was tied to the priest so that if he died in God's presence the other priests could pull him out without having to go in themselves.

Meditate on Hebrews 10:19-23. How has our High Priest rewritten the law about entering the Most Holy Place?

These elaborate precautions were a clear warning: Don't trifle with the holiness of God. Aaron's sons Nadab and Abihu learned that lesson the hard way. When these priests tried a new way of burning incense before the Lord, "fire came out from the presence of the Lord and consumed them, and they died before the Lord" (Lev 10:2). (Needless to say, it was the last time they did anything novel.) In the soberness of that moment, Moses reminded Aaron of the Lord's words: "Among those who approach me I will show myself holy; in the sight of all the people I will be honored" (Lev 10:4). No passage better reflects the Old Testament's central revelation, as summed up by Solomon: "The fear of the Lord is the beginning of knowledge" (Pr 1:7).

> ❝ O sinner, can you give any reason why, since you have risen from your bed this morning, God has not stricken you dead?[10] ❞
> — Jonathan Edwards

Reverence is essential, but we would never get anywhere near the holy presence of God if it weren't for our mediator, Christ Jesus himself. A mediator is one who bridges the gap between two opposing parties. Our sin has alienated and angered God. Yet it hasn't stopped him from loving us. His holiness in no way implies a reluctance on his part to receive us. To the contrary, he took the initiative in sending his Son to put away our sins so that in Christ we might come into his presence and enjoy him forever. As Paul explained to the Corinthians, "God was reconciling the world to himself in Christ" (2Co 5:19). Jesus Christ, as our mediator, suffered the penalty for our disobedience in order to make reconciliation possible. But salvation was the collective desire and cooperative effort of the Father, Son, and Holy Spirit.

Let me offer one final insight from the Old Testament priesthood. It was the priest's responsibility to mediate between God and the people. On each shoulder of the high priest's garment was an onyx stone engraved with the names of six tribes of the nation of Israel. On the breastpiece of his robe were twelve different gemstones, one for each of the twelve tribes. As he entered the Holy of Holies, the priest symbolically bore the people of God on his shoulders and on his heart. In New Testament times, of course, Jesus is our High Priest. So great is his love for us that he also carries us on his shoulders, bearing our burdens, and as our compassionate friend, keeps us close to his heart.

> **❝** The holiness of God teaches us that there is only one way to deal with sin—radically, seriously, painfully, constantly. If you do not so live, you do not live in the presence of the Holy One of Israel.[11] **❞**
>
> **— Sinclair Ferguson**

Meditate on Isaiah 57:15. Why would our holy God choose the second dwelling mentioned in this verse?

Knowing Jesus as our mediator enables us to see God not just as a consuming fire but as a Father to whom we have been reconciled.[12] We ought to apply ourselves to know and appreciate this vital ministry of our Lord Jesus. Comprehending the significance of his priesthood will provoke sincere gratitude and a greater awareness of all that God has done for us.

Ours to Share

One of the most astounding promises in all of Scripture is the assurance that we will share in the holiness of God: "Our fathers disciplined us for a little while as they thought best; but God disciplines us for our good, that we may share in his holiness" (Heb 12:10).

Meditate on 2 Corinthians 7:1. What is our motive for pursuing holiness? What is our method?

When we give serious consideration to our Lord's holiness it seems unbelievable that we could experience some measure of it. But that's what this passage from Hebrews clearly states. As surely as God disciplines his children (and the passage leaves no doubt about that), we will enjoy a portion of his holiness.

That this promise involves discipline should not put us off. Discipline is God's proven method of perfecting his children, and his kind of discipline requires our active participation. This twelfth chapter of Hebrews calls for vigorous effort on our part. Notice the language of exertion the writer employs: "Throw off everything that hinders and the sin that so easily entangles" (v.1)…"run with perseverance the race marked out for us" (v.1)…"In your struggle against sin" (v.4)… "endure hardship" (v.7)… "strengthen your feeble arms and weak knees" (v.12)… "Make every effort to live in peace with all men and to be holy; *without holiness no one will see the Lord*" (v.14, emphasis added). Our Father's discipline may be temporarily painful, but it outfits us for spending eternity with a holy God.

4 All of the spiritual disciplines listed below can help you grow in personal holiness. Check the one discipline in which you feel most deficient.

❏ Bible study

❏ Prayer

❏ Confession/Accountability

❏ Worship

❏ Fasting

❏ Solitude/Rest

Jacob was a man who certainly went through his share of difficulties, many of them self-inflicted. But at the end of his life he was no longer Jacob. His name was Israel. Along the way there had come a name change and a change in character as well. He walked with a limp, leaned on his staff, and worshiped God as the Holy One (Heb 1:21).

Jeremiah said, "It is of the Lord's mercies that we are not consumed" (La 3:22 KJV). We deserve no better treatment than what Nadab and Abihu received. But far from being consumed, we find ourselves the objects of divine love.

Perhaps nowhere is this more clearly illustrated than in the circumstances surrounding the conversion of Saul of Tarsus. He was a zealous persecutor of the early church, responsible for the deaths of many men and women who were followers of Jesus Christ. While Saul was on an official journey to Damascus to ferret out and punish Christians, the Lord himself dramatically intervened and put a stop to his activities. In recounting the incident to King Agrippa years later, Paul said:

For Further Study:
Read how Aaron led the Israelites in idolatry while Moses was meeting with God (Ex 32:1-10, 19-28). Contrast that with God's eventual consecration of Aaron as high priest (Ex 39:27-31, 40:12-16). Did Aaron get what he deserved?

"About noon, O king, as I was on the road, I saw a light from heaven, brighter than the sun, blazing around me and my companions. We all fell to the ground, and I heard a voice saying to me in Aramaic, 'Saul, Saul, why do you persecute me? It is hard for you to kick against the goads.' Then I asked, 'Who are you, Lord?' 'I am Jesus, whom you are persecuting,' the Lord replied. 'Now get up and stand on your feet. I have appeared to you to appoint you as a servant and as a witness of what you have seen of me and what I will show you'" (Ac 26:13-16).

It's fascinating that Saul emerged from this encounter alive. God would have been completely justified in destroying him right there on the Damascus road. But instead of receiving justice at the hands of the holy One he was persecuting, Saul experienced the Lord's great love and acceptance. He even received a commission to serve as ambassador for the One he had so vehemently opposed. What amazing grace!

God's holiness does indeed set him apart from us, as far as the heavens are above the earth. But thank God, it has not prevented him from reaching down and turning Jacobs into Israels and Sauls into Pauls. Our names may never change, but our internal transformation is guaranteed as we encounter the holiness of God. ∎

GROUP DISCUSSION

1. How would you define blasphemy? Give examples of how Christians as well as non-Christians blaspheme God.

2. According to the author, why did God consecrate so many things as holy in the Old Testament?

3. Of all the disciples, John was most intimate with Jesus. In light of that, what is significant about John's reaction to his vision of Jesus in Revelation 1:10-17?

4. Has God's holiness caused you personally to experience the "disintegration factor"? (Page 29)

5. Which of God's attributes do you find most attractive? Most intimidating?

6. What types of behavior might indicate that a Christian has become overly familiar with God?

7. Do you think it's *fair* for God to execute someone?

8. Which spiritual discipline did you pick in Question 4 on this page? How could you develop that discipline?

9. What level of holiness can we expect in this life?

10. Did this chapter's discussion of holiness make you scared of God or secure in him?

RECOMMENDED READING

Holiness by J.C. Ryle (Hertfordshire, England: Evangelical Press, 1979. Originally published in 1879.)

The Holiness of God by R.C. Sproul (Wheaton, IL: Tyndale House Publishers, 1985)

The Knowledge of the Holy by A.W. Tozer (Camp Hill, PA: Christian Publications, Inc., 1978)

CHAPTER FOUR

THE WRATH OF GOD

C.J. MAHANEY

A wildly popular topic in Christian literature today is "self-esteem." By contrast, the subject of sin is often overlooked, or even challenged head-on. To call sin rebellion against God is "shallow and insulting to the human being," writes one Christian author. As much as I appreciate this individual's sincerity, I am deeply concerned about the perspective he and many others are advocating. It's unbiblical. It hinders us from understanding the seriousness of sin, the reality of wrath, and the necessity of the Cross.

Jesus did not go to the Cross to set us free from low self-esteem, but from something far more serious: the wrath of God and the presence, power, and penalty of sin (in which pride, or *excess* self-esteem, plays a huge role in all our lives).

To understand how amazing grace is we must understand the seriousness of sin. To appreciate God's love necessitates understanding his wrath. Though anything but flattering, a realistic appraisal of our own sinfulness—and its horrifying consequences—is an essential step as we explore the doctrine of justification.

For Further Study:
Enhance an *accurate* view of your self-image (and shatter your self-esteem) by reviewing 1Kings 8:46, Jeremiah 17:9, Romans 3:10-18, 23, and 1John 1:8.

A Glimpse in the Rearview Mirror

"If anyone is in Christ, he is a new creation; the old has gone, the new has come!" (2Co 5:17). Meditating on the miracle of regeneration gives us real cause to rejoice. Unless we occasionally look in our rearview mirror, however, remembering what we were before God in his mercy regenerated us, our celebration will be superficial. As Martin Luther once said, "A person must confront his own sinfulness in all its ravaging depths before he can enjoy the comforts of salvation."

1 If you were the self-appointed campaign manager for Jesus' "Messiah A.D. '32" bid, which of the following would you edit out of his speeches?

❏ "If anyone comes to me and does not hate his father and mother, his wife and children, his brothers and sisters—yes, even his own life—he cannot be my disciple." (Lk 14:26)

❏ "No one who puts his hand to the plow and looks back is fit for service in the kingdom of God." (Lk 9:62)

❏ "Blessed are you when people insult you, persecute you and falsely say all kinds of evil against you because of me." (Mt 5:11)

❏ "Let the dead bury their own dead, but you go and proclaim the kingdom of God." (Lk 9:60)

❏ "It is easier for a camel to go through the eye of a needle than for a rich man to enter the kingdom of God." (Mt 19:24)

❏ "Do not suppose that I have come to bring peace to the earth. I did not come to bring peace, but a sword." (Mt 10:34)

❏ "If someone strikes you on the right cheek, turn to him the other also. If someone forces you to go one mile, go with him two miles." (Mt 5:39,41)

(Aren't you glad that Jesus wasn't a politician?)

Meditate on Romans 1:28-32. This passage doesn't refer to a select group of the world's worst sinners—it describes the natural state of every person apart from regeneration. See also Ephesians 2:1-3.

In one short verse Paul summarizes the enmity that existed between us and God prior to conversion: "Once you were alienated from God and were enemies in your minds because of your evil behavior" (Col 1:21). The absolute necessity and remarkable benefits of justification should come into focus as we dissect this sobering verse.

Alienated from God. Paul expands this description in his letter to the Ephesian church: "Remember that at that time you were separate from Christ...foreigners to the covenants of the promise, without hope and without God in the world" (Eph 2:12). We were alienated from God without any sensitivity concerning the reality of sin. As Peter T. O'Brien has stated, we were "continuously and persistently out of harmony with God."[1]

Now I doubt you were "continuously and persistently" *aware* of your alienation at the time. Before I was converted I was totally unaware of my estrangement from God. Avidly committed to the partying lifestyle, I was enjoying the passing pleasures of sin. I had little knowledge of or interest in God.

Whether we sensed the separation or not at the time, Scripture states that every individual has a desperate need to be reconciled to God. Our alienation was absolute. Had it not been for God's merciful intervention, we would have been separated from him for eternity. There was nothing we could have done to alter that alienated state.

Enemies in your mind. A persistent and popular rumor has been circulating for several thousand years now which says man is essentially good. Sure we make mistakes, but overall we're pretty decent folks. Anyone who believes that myth isn't paying attention. As Paul states so clearly to the Colossians, we weren't God's allies or even neutral observers. R.C. Lucas says we were "antagonistic, not merely apathetic."[3] Theologian Anthony Hoekema makes the point well in this statement: "Sin is

> **❝** We have a strange illusion that mere time cancels sin. I have heard others and I have heard myself recounting cruelties and falsehoods committed in my boyhood as if they were no concern of the present speakers, and even with laughter, but mere time does nothing either to the fact or the guilt of sin.[2] **❞**
>
> **— C.S. Lewis**

For Further Study:
Read Romans 1:18-21. Can those who have never heard the gospel or read the Bible be accused of being God's enemies?

2 List one or two things you did before becoming a Christian that you would consider good. Then, read Psalm 14:2-3 and Isaiah 64:6, and briefly summarize God's perspective of your "good" deeds.

therefore fundamentally opposition to God, rebellion against God, which roots in hatred of God."[4]

Prior to your conversion you hated God. So did I. Don't flatter or deceive yourself by entertaining any thought to the contrary. You won't appreciate that you love him now if you don't realize you hated him then.

Evil in your behavior. We associate the word "evil" with the kind of atrocities that Saddam Hussein or Adolf Hitler might commit. Yet anything that challenges or rejects God's authority is evil. To sin means to defy or disobey the moral law of God. It can involve motive, attitude, or actions. From God's perspective, even our "best" behavior is to some degree evil.

The moment we commit a sin it enters the unalterable past. Our record is permanently flawed. And eventually that record will be reviewed by Almighty God.

"At one time or another," says R.C. Sproul, "we all have been struck by the sobering thought that one day each of us will stand in the presence of God to be judged. The fear that arises from such a prospect stems from our awareness that based on our own merit we will never hear the verdict 'not guilty.'"[5] Our past will accuse us for having directly assaulted—time after time after time—the authority of God. We will be without excuse. And merciful though he is, God in his justice will not overlook or ignore our rebellion. He will hold us responsible.

Are you so familiar with your status as a new creation that you've forgotten what you were apart from Christ? Do you realize what it means to be spared the wrath of God? Meditating on our sin and God's wrath won't lead to condemnation; rather, it will lead to an intense appreciation of what Jesus accomplished on the Cross. If you've never been struck by your own unworthiness, I doubt you sufficiently comprehend or appreciate the grace of God. I'd respectfully question whether you even know him at all.

Stuck in the Stone Age

God's wrath is not a fashionable topic of conversation among this generation of upbeat baby boomers obsessed with their own self-improvement. I have yet to hear of Oprah Winfrey devoting airtime to the wrath of God. Our culture doesn't take it seriously. It's seen as a primitive notion. What's frightening, though, is the fact that the Church so often relates to the subject in a similar way. In numerous churches God's wrath is never mentioned. Many theologians have dismissed it. Embarrassed by such stone-age concepts as hell and torment, we downplay and doubt their existence. The most common result is an over-emphasis on God's love without a corresponding emphasis on his holiness and his wrath.

While falling all over ourselves trying to conceal this "embarrassing" feature of God's character, we've sent this signal to our culture: God is infinitely understanding, sympathetic, patient, and sentimental. God is nice! God is a kind of cosmic Mr. Rogers, always ready to greet you with a warm smile and a pleasant word.

Because we have difficulty reconciling wrath with our perception of a loving God, the Church and this culture have sought to create God in their own image. But Scripture makes no apologies concerning the wrath of God. In fact, A.W. Pink notes that there are more references to God's wrath in the Bible than to his love. We probably don't have many of these passages underlined, but perhaps we should. We need to give serious study to the wrath of God.

Paul and other biblical writers had no inhibitions about expressing God's wrath. Why? Because they knew that understanding the fix of justification begins with understanding the reality of God's wrath. Unless you are aware of the certainty of wrath, you won't

Meditate on Romans 11:22. Can you accept the fact that God has such contrasting traits? How does he demonstrate each of these characteristics?

3 Each of the Scripture references below describes a particular aspect of torment in hell. In the space next to each verse, name the condition each reveals.

Example:
- Job 18:17-19 *Utter worthlessness*

- Jude 13_____

- Revelation 21: _____

- Luke 16:24_____

- Matthew 22:13 _____

- Revelation 14:11_____

- Daniel 12:2 _____

(Answers printed upside down at bottom of page 43.)

> **"** The most destructive myth of twentieth-century American religion is...that there is no wrath in God. Nothing promotes godlessness more than that myth.[7] **"**
>
> — R.C. Sproul

For Further Study:
To see what the Bible says about hell, look up Matthew 3:12, 5:22, and 26:41, Mark 9:47-49, Luke 3:17, and 2 Peter 2:4.

understand the necessity of justification. Without wrath, mercy is meaningless. Without wrath, grace is unnecessary. Without wrath, you have no gospel. Without wrath, you'll never feel the need to be justified before Almighty God.

It's difficult to communicate effectively about God's wrath. Some people seem to enjoy describing the horrors that await unrepentant sinners. That's not God's attitude and it shouldn't be ours. Your local newspaper and the network news probably aren't going to investigate the subject of wrath—at least not in a biblical way—so let's examine what Scripture has to say on this topic.

When Sin and Holiness Collide

Jack Kevorkian was dubbed "Doctor Death" by the media for using a special device to assist people in suicide. I can't forget the time I saw a video clip of Kevorkian and two women made just before they took their lives. These ladies were unusually calm. As they spoke of their desire to end their lives, I felt grief and a sense of horror. They had no idea what lay beyond death. Unwilling to face the diseases that were afflicting their bodies, they unsuspectingly subjected their souls to the wrath of God.

God's wrath is real. It's terrifying. When his holiness and our sin collide, the inevitable result is wrath, which J.I. Packer defines as "God's resolute action in punishing sin."

God is not indulgent, nor is he merely indignant over our sin. His wrath makes a Stephen King horror novel look like a nursery rhyme. The more you get to know him, the more your fear of him will increase. And that's good. If this generation were to take a crash course in the fear of God, our shallow view of sin would immediately deepen.

> **"** It is partly because sin does not provoke our own wrath that we do not believe that sin provokes the wrath of God.[8] **"**
>
> — R.W. Dale

The prophet Habakkuk says of God, "Your eyes are too pure to look on evil; you cannot tolerate wrong" (Hab 1:13). In expressing God's pending judgment against Nineveh, Nahum prophesied,

Meditate on Exodus 20:18-20. Moses describes "the fear of God" as a good thing, but urges the people not to be afraid of God. Can you see the difference?

The Lord is a jealous and avenging God; the Lord takes vengeance and is filled with wrath. The Lord takes vengeance on his foes and maintains his wrath against his enemies. The Lord is slow to anger and great in power; the Lord will not leave the guilty unpunished...

Who can withstand his indignation? Who can endure his fierce anger? His wrath is poured out like fire; the rocks are shattered before him. The Lord is good, a refuge in times of trouble. He cares for those who trust in him, but with an overwhelming flood he will make an end of Nineveh; he will pursue his foes into darkness. (Na 1:2-3,6-8)

God's wrath wasn't limited to Nineveh. Though he demonstrates unbelievable patience and is "slow to anger," our sins provoke his wrath as well. If we reject God's goodness that has been offered through the person and finished work of Jesus Christ, we will one day experience his severity, and we will have no one to blame but ourselves.

Meditate on Psalm 78:38-39. What should surprise us about God is not that he has wrath, but that he so often restrains himself from unleashing that wrath.

God didn't communicate his wrath just through a few minor prophets in some brief and obscure sections of the Old Testament. Paul writes in the first chapter of Romans, "The wrath of God is being revealed from heaven against all the godlessness and wickedness of men who suppress the truth by their wickedness" (v.18). God's wrath was a present reality in Paul's day, and is in ours as well. You don't have to wonder if America will one day be judged. America is *already* experiencing the wrath of God. When individuals call right wrong and wrong right, when immoral and idolatrous lifestyles become the norm, know that these are manifestations of wrath. One of the most effective and terrifying forms of judgment occurs when God ceases to intervene on our behalf. He simply withdraws and says in effect, "I will leave you to yourselves and allow you to experience the consequences of your rebellion."

God doesn't have to destroy us directly; all he has to do is remove his hand and we destroy ourselves.

God's anger is not like the anger of man. He doesn't have a bad temper. This isn't some undisciplined basketball coach throwing a tantrum on the sidelines. God's anger is just. It is neither arbitrary nor unpredictable. Rather, it is a premeditated and measured response to our godlessness and wickedness. Those things make God angry. And he will express it! Those who receive God's wrath deserve it! They have no one to blame but themselves.

You may be thinking to yourself, "That's not my God you're describing," but this *is* the God revealed in the Bible. Though rarely discussed among Christians today, wrath and justice are very much a part of his character. His anger is fully appropriate, for if he were not angry at sin he would not be morally perfect. God's wrath is as real as his love, and that fact places the unregenerated in a serious, desperate state.

Before closing this section, let me insert one final point. What was the primary purpose of the Cross? Just this: It was there that Jesus satisfied the fierce and holy wrath of Almighty God which we would otherwise have experienced. God's accumulated and justified anger fell, in all its power and severity, not on us who deserved it, but on his Son. Jesus didn't just save us from our sin—he saved us from God himself.

"We were by nature objects of wrath," wrote Paul (Eph 2:3). God could and should have judged us for our rebellion against his rule. Instead he extended grace. At the Cross he found a way to reconcile his perfect justice and perfect mercy. The very One opposed to us while we were in our sin died in our place so that we, his enemies, might be adopted into his family.

> **"** There is not only a wicked opposition of the sinner to God, but a holy opposition of God to the sinner. **"**
>
> **— Charles Hodge**

Jonathan Edwards was an instrumental force behind America's first Great Awakening in the mid-eighteenth century. He is perhaps best known for a message he delivered titled "Sinners in the Hands of An Angry God." According to eyewitness accounts, various members of Edwards' congregation were so dramatically affected by the message that they clutched their seats, fell on their knees, and cried out in anguish at the prospect of their own damnation.

This was no stereotypical "fire and brimstone" tirade, however. From what I understand the listeners were not influenced by pulpit-banging or wild-eyed shouting, because there wasn't any—Edwards read the message in a monotone. And while painting a clear picture of divine wrath, he placed primary emphasis on the gracious hands of God, for as Edwards was well aware, when we encounter the reality of wrath we gain fresh desire and appreciation for grace.

Answers: Jude 13 (absolute darkness), Rev 21:8 (fire and burning), Lk 16:24 (thirst), Mt 22:13 (weeping/gnashing of teeth), Rev 14:11 (sleeplessness), Da 12:2 (shame and contempt).

43

God's wrath is real, terrifying, inevitable. But his nail-pierced hands are open and full of mercy. All who humble themselves in awe at the Cross will be spared the wrath to come.

Unfelt Needs

Not long ago a nationwide Gallup poll revealed that an increasing number of Americans consider themselves "born again." It's a bit premature to start celebrating, though, because the Church's impact on this culture is not keeping pace with the statistics. If the percentage of Americans calling themselves Christians were authentic disciples of Jesus Christ, our society would undergo radical reform.

Contributing to this problem is the fact that people are supposedly getting converted without an awareness of sin. Rather than confronting individuals with the reality of God's wrath, evangelism has degenerated into a sales job. Rather than clarifying the horror of man's sinful condition and his desperate need for Christ, the gospel has been re-packaged as a slick set of benefits targeted to address specific "felt needs."

But leading people to conversion without first exposing them to the extent of their own sin and God's wrath is truly a terrible disservice. Countless converts come too quickly to the solution without fully understanding the problem. They don't realize how they have violated God's perfect law and don't feel the justified wrath of God upon their lives. As a result, because they have not fathomed the amazing grace of Almighty God, they end up uncertain of his love.

You won't enjoy describing God's wrath to others, and they won't enjoy it either. Who likes to hear that he is a God-hating sinner? It's much easier to focus exclusively on the love of God. Yet the gospel is incomplete without an emphasis on wrath, for this is what puts God's love in perspective. We were alienated from him, enemies in our minds, characterized by evil behavior, and objects of wrath. He had every right to waste us without explanation

> 66 Our evangelical emphasis on the atonement is dangerous if we come to it too quickly. We learn to appreciate the access to God which Christ has won for us only after we have first seen God's inaccessibility to the sinner. We can cry 'hallelujah' with authenticity only after we have first cried 'woe is me, for I am lost.'"[9] 99
>
> — John Stott

For Further Study:
Read the text of Peter's Pentecost message that resulted in 3,000 conversions (Ac 2:14-41). Notice verses 23, 36, and 40 in particular. Could Peter's style be considered "seeker sensitive"?

or apology. Instead, he gave up his only beloved Son to suffer judgment in our place. Apart from a revelation of wrath, we will never appreciate the absolute necessity of justification.

We must get back to a biblical presentation of and response to the gospel. We must make people aware of their most significant and serious need, a need they probably don't even feel: deliverance from the justified wrath of God. We must remind them (and remind ourselves) that though his anger is slow, it is certain. We must explain that, as the Bible makes so clear, "It is a dreadful thing to fall into the hands of the living God" without having been justified by Jesus Christ (Heb 10:31).

> ❝ In today's world there is little emphasis on the biblical doctrine of sin. But a person with a shallow sense of sin and of the wrath of God against our sin will neither feel the need for nor understand the biblical doctrine of justification.[10] ❞
>
> — **Anthony Hoekema**

As I read Jonathan Edwards' message I find myself thinking, *No wonder there was a revival! No wonder the power of God accompanied this teaching. No wonder there was unprecedented conviction during that period of time.* Without minimizing the sovereign move of the Holy Spirit which made the Great Awakening so fruitful, I would submit that the content of the preaching had a great deal to do with it as well. When the Church again gives equal weight to wrath and mercy in its proclamation of the gospel, then individuals will be converted with a profound appreciation of grace. Rather than blend in with the culture they will stand out as radically different. They'll be able to relate to it, but no longer will they reflect it. Instead, thanks to an authentic conversion, they will increasingly reflect the character of God.

Meditate on 2 Thessalonians 1:5-9. What stands out most to you in this vivid description of judgment?

Never Lose Touch

Theologian R.C. Sproul describes an interesting encounter he had with a zealous but tactless believer. The man suddenly confronted him one day as he was walking across a college campus.

"Are you saved?" the man demanded without even introducing himself. Sproul was startled and a bit offended by the man's approach.

"Saved from what?" he shot back.

Now it was the would-be evangelist's turn to be startled. He became confused and was unable to give a specific response. He probably went away sensing a need for further Bible study...and a need to select his evangelistic targets more carefully.

"Saved" is a familiar word in our Christian vocabulary, but Sproul's question deserves a thoughtful response: From what have we been saved? By this point in the chapter you've probably anticipated the answer. We haven't been saved from low self-esteem. We have been saved "from the wrath to come" (1Th 1:10).

Our ignorance of wrath isn't purely coincidental. I believe we avoid the topic because it makes us feel frightened and condemned. There's truth to that—we should be frightened because we deserve to be condemned. But a study of wrath leads to an understanding of grace and a release from condemnation. As much as we deserved eternal damnation, God saved us from his wrath and reconciled us to himself!

> ❝ Divine love triumphed over divine wrath by divine self-sacrifice.[11] ❞
> — John Stott

Rehearsing and reviewing your past won't drag you down into a pit of bleak introspection. Instead, it will lift your understanding of God and his mercy to new heights. You will comprehend the greatness of God's love in a dimension you never have before.

Meditate on Psalm 103:1-18. Nothing provokes worship more than the realization that God "does not treat us as our sins deserve or repay us according to our iniquities."

In his commentary on our Scripture passage from Colossians, Peter T. O'Brien says of the church at Colossae, "The gravity of their previous condition serves to magnify the wonder of God's mercy. The past is recalled not because the emphasis falls upon it, but to draw attention to God's mighty action...on the reader's behalf."[12] We don't recall the past in order to remain in it—we look back so that God's mighty action on our behalf through the justifying work of his Son can transform our lives in the dramatic way he intends. That was the case with Paul. He never lost touch with his past. In fact, look at the benefit he gained from a little retrospection:

> Christ Jesus came into the world to save sinners—of whom I am the worst. But for that very reason I was shown mercy so that in me, the worst of sinners, Christ Jesus might display his unlimited patience as an example for those who would believe on him and receive eternal life. Now to the King eternal,

immortal, invisible, the only God, be honor and glory for ever and ever. Amen. (1Ti 1:15-17)

Did looking back send Paul into a state of depression? No—it provoked a spontaneous outburst of worship for the wonder of God's grace. "Once you were alienated from God," Paul wrote, "and were enemies in your minds because of your evil behavior." Then he uses one of the smallest yet most beautiful words in the Bible: "**But** now he has reconciled you by Christ's physical body through death to present you holy in his sight, without blemish and free from accusation" (Co 1:21-22).

> **❝** The glory of the gospel is this: The one from whom we need to be saved is the one who has saved us. **❞**
>
> — R.C. Sproul

Rather than leaving us in our hopeless, helpless, desperate state, God reconciled us through Jesus so that we could stand in his presence without blemish and free from accusation—in a word, justified. We deserved eternal torment in hell. Instead he gave us eternal life through his Son.

Is that good news, or what? ■

GROUP DISCUSSION

1. Did this chapter affect your self-esteem? Your self-image?

2. "Prior to your conversion you hated God," says the author (Page 39). Do you agree or disagree?

3. Nineteenth-century atheist Colonel Robert Ingersoll once said, "The idea of hell was born of revenge and brutality on the one side, and cowardice on the other...I have no respect for any human being who believes in it...I dislike this doctrine, I hate it, I despise it, I defy this doctrine." If given the chance, how would you answer Colonel Ingersoll?

4. According to the author, what's the missing ingredient in contemporary evangelism? (Page 44)

5. Is it possible to fear God without being afraid of him? Explain your answer.

6. How does God's anger differ from our anger?

7. On page 44 the author writes, "Countless converts come too quickly to the solution without fully understanding the problem." What does he mean?

8. Why does God send sinners to hell when he could show mercy by forgiving them?

9. How can an awareness of God's wrath deepen our sense of security in his love? Was that your experience in this chapter?

RECOMMENDED READING

Knowing God by J.I. Packer (Downers Grove, IL: InterVarsity Press, 1973)

The Atonement by Leon Morris (Downwers Grove, IL: InterVarsity Press, 1984)

The Holiness of God by R.C. Sproul (Wheaton, IL: Tyndale House Publishers, 1985)

CHAPTER FIVE

JUSTIFIED BY CHRIST

C.J. MAHANEY

Before Martin Luther became famous for his pivotal role in the Reformation, he was known throughout Europe as a brilliant student of law. What affected this Augustinian monk most was his study of God's law in Scripture. As he meditated on the commands of God, he became very aware of the wrath of God. Whenever he studied the person and work of Jesus Christ he knew that this was the righteous One who would ultimately judge him.

That persistent realization plagued Luther with an overwhelming sense of guilt. While his contemporaries spent minutes confessing their sin, he spent hours. Some thought he was mentally unstable.

Theologian Anthony Hoekema describes the mental anguish leading up to Luther's great theological discovery:

> Martin Luther had tried everything: sleeping on hard floors, going without food, even climbing a staircase in Rome on his hands and knees—but to no avail. His teachers at the monastery told him that he was doing enough to have peace of soul. But he had no peace. His sense of sin was too deep.
>
> He had been studying the Psalms. They often mentioned "the righteousness of God." But this term bothered him. He thought it meant God's punitive righteousness, whereby he punishes sinners. And Luther knew that he was a sinner. So when he saw the word *righteousness* in the Bible, he saw red.
>
> One day he opened to the Book of Romans. There he read about the gospel of Christ which is the power of God for salvation (1:16). This was good news! But the next verse said, "For therein is the righteousness of God revealed"—there was that bad

> **"** Justification is indeed God's answer to the most important of all human questions: How can a man or a woman become right with God? We are not right with God in ourselves. We are under God's wrath. Justification is vital, because we must become right with God or perish eternally ...The difficulty is that most people today do not actually feel a need in this area. Martin Luther did; it is what haunted him. He knew he was not right with God, and he anticipated a confrontation with an angry God at the final judgment. God showed him that he could experience a right relationship with God through the work of Jesus Christ. But who feels the intensity of Luther's anguish today?[1] **"**
>
> **— James Montgomery Boice**

word *righteousness* again! And Luther's depression returned. It got worse when he went on to read about the wrath of God revealed from heaven against all the unrighteousness of men (v.18).

So Luther again turned to verse 17. How could Paul have written such terrible words?...Suddenly the light dawned on him. The "righteousness of God" Paul here had in mind was not God's punitive justice which leads him to punish sinners, but rather a righteousness which God *gives* to the needy sinner, and which that sinner accepts by *faith*. This was a spotless and perfect righteousness, earned by Christ, which God graciously bestows on all who believe. No longer did Luther need to seek the basis for peace of soul in himself, in his own good works. Now he could look away from himself to Christ, and live by faith instead of groveling in fear. At that moment, the Protestant Reformation was born.[2]

Meditate on Romans 1:17. What key phrase in this verse revolutionized Martin Luther's understanding of salvation? How does it affect you?

Luther would go on to say that the doctrine of justification is the article by which the Church stands or falls. "This article is the head and cornerstone of the Church which alone begets, nourishes, builds, and protects the Church. Without it the church of God could not subsist for one hour."[3] At another point he added, "If the article of justification be once lost, then is all true Christian doctrine lost."[4]

Luther's fear of God's wrath was justified, as we learned in the previous chapter. All Christians need to remember who and what they once were: evil in their behavior, enemies of God, completely alienated from him, and objects of his wrath. But identifying with the past has value only to the extent that it makes us more aware of and amazed about our present position in Christ. We must recognize who we *now are* by God's gracious gift of justification.

Those who have received Christ's justifying work have

experienced a dramatic, extraordinary change. We have been justified by faith through the amazing grace of Almighty God. Without an accurate and experiential knowledge of justification the Church "could not subsist for one hour"…at least not with any degree of authenticity. Neither could we.

Position or Process?

Justification is a legal term that means "to pronounce or declare righteous." Hoekema defines justification as "a permanent change in our judicial relation to God whereby we are absolved from the charge of guilt, and whereby God forgives all our sins on the basis of the finished work of Jesus Christ."[5] Though we are guilty before the holy Judge of all, having violated his law and deserving his wrath, he has declared us righteous. How? On the basis of what Jesus Christ accomplished on the Cross. Only the Cross can make us acceptable before God.

Justification is a gift we receive from God, not something we achieve or accomplish. We aren't responsible or capable of contributing to our justification before God. This righteous status cannot be earned or deserved, only accepted and appreciated. We receive what Christ and Christ alone has accomplished for us.

In order to fully understand this breathtaking truth, it's essential that we differentiate between justification and sanctification. Although these two doctrines are inseparable, we must distinguish between their respective roles in the life of faith.

Justification means we are *declared* righteous. Sanctification means we are being *made* righteous. (Comprehend that difference alone and your life will never be the same!) Justification is the *gift* of righteousness; sanctification is the *practice* of righteousness. Perhaps most critically, justification is a *position* —established immediately and completely upon conversion—whereas sanctification is a *process* of internal change and character development that begins at regeneration and continues as long as we live. "In Scripture," writes Sinclair Ferguson, "to justify does not mean to make righteous in the sense of changing a person's character. It means to constitute

For Further Study: At the moment Jesus died on the Cross, the temple curtain separating the Holy Place from the Most Holy Place was supernaturally ripped in two. To understand the awesome significance of that act, read Hebrews 9:1-14.

> **❝** Nobody has understood Christianity who does not understand this word. It is the word "justified."[6] **❞**
>
> — **John Stott**

> **❝** Justification is an ACT. It is not a work, or series of acts. It is not progressive. The weakest believer and the strongest saint are alike and equally justified. Justification admits no degrees. A man is either wholly justified or wholly condemned in the sight of God.[8] **❞**
> — **William S. Plumer**

righteous and to do so by declaration."[7]

Justification isn't a process. It is a declaration, a divine decree which cannot be challenged, altered, or appealed. Paul emphatically states, "Therefore since we *have been* justified through faith, we have peace with God through our Lord Jesus Christ" (Ro 5:1, emphasis added). This glorious transformation doesn't take place by degrees, nor does it fluctuate. You're not more justified during certain periods than you are at others. You'll never be more justified than you are at this time. That's worth repeating: *You'll never be more justified than you are at this time.* To top it off, no one in history has ever been more justified than you are now. Not Martin Luther, not Paul—nobody.

Numerous Christians confuse the doctrines of justification and sanctification and are subsequently robbed of the full benefits this great salvation entails. It is imperative that we understand the difference between our position (justification) and our practice (sanctification). While sanctification is both the *evidence* and *objective* of our justification, it should never be viewed as the *grounds* for our justification before God, regardless of how mature we become. We are incapable of adding to what Christ has accomplished. As Alister McGrath states, "The only thing we could really be said to contribute to our justification is the sin God so graciously forgives." We are justified by grace alone.[9]

1 Have you been robbed of the benefits of your great salvation? Take the following True/False quiz to make sure you fully understand the difference between justification and sanctification.

(Answers printed upside down at bottom of page.)

- Justification is the by-product of sanctification.   **T   F**

- Sanctification is a life-long process.   **T   F**

- God's love for us grows in proportion to our maturity.   **T   F**

- Justification refers to our position in Christ; sanctification refers to a process.   **T   F**

- Breaking sinful habits makes us more righteous.   **T   F**

- Spiritual growth is good evidence that we've been justified.   **T   F**

Frustrating and Futile

The doctrine of justification needs to be constantly reinforced and reviewed, as Martin Luther was well aware. His typically blunt advice? "Beat it into their heads continually."[10] In addition to such persistent repetition from

Answers: F, T, F, T, F, T

52

our leaders, we need to be applying and appreciating the truth of justification in our lives on a daily basis. If we don't, we will find ourselves susceptible to one of the Church's most subtle and serious enemies: legalism.

Legalism involves seeking to earn God's acceptance through our own obedience. We only have two options: either receive righteousness as a God-given gift or try to generate our own. Legalism is the attempt to be justified through some source other than Jesus Christ and his finished work.

> **"** The glory of the gospel is that God has declared Christians to be rightly related to him in spite of their sin. But our greatest temptation and mistake is to try to smuggle character into his work of grace. How easily we fall into the trap of assuming that we only remain justified so long as there are grounds in our character for that justification. But Paul's teaching is that nothing we do ever contributes to our justification.[11] **"**
>
> **— Sinclair Ferguson**

To adhere to legalism is to believe that the Cross was either unnecessary or insufficient (Gal 2:21, 5:2). That is an accurate interpretation of your motive and actions, even if you still ascribe mentally to the necessity of Christ's sacrifice. In our legitimate pursuit of obedience and maturity legalism slowly and subtly overtakes us, and we begin to substitute our works for his finished work. The result is either arrogance or condemnation. Instead of growing in grace we abandon grace. That was Paul's assessment of the Galatian church when he wrote, "You who are trying to be justified by law have been alienated from Christ; you have fallen away from grace" (Gal 5:4).

For Further Study: To appreciate the extent of Paul's concern about legalism, read Galatians 1:6-9, 2:21, 3:1-4, 3:10, 4:8-11, 4:19-20, 5:2-4, and 5:7-12.

If you've ever attempted to live this way you may have learned by now that legalism is as futile as it is frustrating. Every legalistic attempt at righteousness inevitably ends in failure. Over the years I've learned to recognize some unmistakable signs of the presence of legalism. Here are a few of them:

■ You are more aware of your past sin than of the person and finished work of Christ.

■ You live thinking, believing, and feeling that God is disappointed with you rather than delighting in you. You assume God's acceptance depends on your obedience.

■ You lack joy. This is often the first indication of the presence of legalism. Condemnation is the result of pondering our deficiency; joy is the result of considering his sufficiency.

Have you been ensnared by the subtle presence of legalism? If so, beware. It tends to spread rather than remain restricted (Gal 5:9). Legalism must be removed.

The only effective way to uproot legalism is with the doctrine of justification. If you've neglected or ignored this doctrine, then take whatever dramatic action is necessary to change. Set aside time each day to review, rehearse, and rejoice in this great, objective, positional truth. Restrict your spiritual diet to the study of justification until you are certain of God's acceptance, secure in his love, and free from legalism and condemnation.

The crucifixion of Jesus Christ was the single most decisive event in history. Accurately has Sinclair Ferguson stated the following:

Meditate on Romans 7:14-25. Once we come to grips with our own wretchedness we'll find it much harder to be tempted by legalism.

> When we think of Christ dying on the Cross we are shown the lengths to which God's love goes in order to win us back to himself...He is saying to us: I love you this much...The Cross is the heart of the gospel. It makes the gospel good news: Christ died for us. He has stood in our place before God's judgment seat. He has borne our sins. God has done something on the Cross we could never do for ourselves...The reason we lack assurance of his grace is because we fail to focus on that spot where he has revealed it.[13]

Where will you focus your attention? Will it be on past sin, your present emotional state, or areas of character in which you still need to grow? Or will you focus on the finished work of Christ? Legalism need not motivate you. Condemnation need not torment you. God has justified you.

Don't Argue with the Judge

Intellectually understanding the doctrine of justification is in itself insufficient. God intends that we be transformed—totally, genuinely, and permanently transformed by this central doctrine. J.I. Packer has insightfully stated, "The issue is not, can one state the doctrine with full biblical accuracy (that, as we have seen, is a task that demands care), but, does one know its reality in experience."[14]

For Further Study: What two categories of people are described in James 1:22-25? Which group does God promise to bless?

Our goal in writing this book is not primarily that you learn how to articulate this great doctrine but that you be *changed* by it, that your understanding results in personal freedom from legalism and condemnation as well as an

2 Colossians 2:13-15 reveals the enormous debt we owed God. What did Jesus do to the law's "invoice"?

ever-increasing passion and love for Jesus Christ. It's possible to be aware of justification by grace without being personally affected. We need to appreciate and apply this magnificent truth each and every day.

The story I'm about to relate has been a powerful lesson for me as I have sought to appropriate the doctrine of justification. During my pre-conversion days as a college freshman I was arrested for possession of marijuana. The details of the trial are still vivid in my mind. As I sat in the courtroom facing the judge, I tried my best to look both sincere and sorrowful, but I was just scared. I knew there was an excellent chance that I would be convicted and even charged with additional violations.

As it turned out, my case never progressed beyond the first witness. Because officials had searched my dorm room without the necessary legal documents, argued my lawyer, the court would have to drop the charge.

> **"** It is never enough to know simply that Christ died, or even why he died. Such knowledge is the result of a "merely historical faith" that cannot save...Only when we realize that Christ was given *pro me, pro nobis* ("for me," "for us") have we discerned the import of Christ's accomplishment.[15] **"**
>
> — **Timothy George**

The judge sat listening stoically as the prosecution objected and reiterated the evidence against me. Finally, he looked down at me. The man was obviously frustrated. Powerless to give anything more than a reprimand, he lectured me in the strongest possible terms.

I tried to appear contrite. I nodded my head at each statement. But I don't remember a thing he said—I was too excited about the fact that he was going to let me go.

When I stood trial I knew I was guilty. I think everyone knew. But when the judge released me I didn't argue with him. I didn't appeal and plead with the judge to continue the case. I didn't request that he overlook the legal technicality and allow the prosecution to proceed. For once, I gladly deferred to someone with greater authority. If the judge wanted to dismiss the violation, I would happily accept his decision.

Each of us stands guilty before the Judge of all. But our crime against him is in a totally different league than my misdemeanor. And though I escaped on a technicality, we have been declared righteous on the basis of Christ's pre-

Meditate on Deuteronomy 31:8.
Rather than break this wonderful promise to us (even though we never deserved such a guarantee), God forsook his own Son.

meditated and substitutionary sacrifice. Jesus Christ voluntarily and purposefully laid down his life so God could remain just while justifying the guilty—you and me. God has declared us righteous. All that remains is the issue of whether or not we will receive this pronouncement. The choice confronts us daily, often multiple times in a given day: Will we receive justification by faith because of the declaration by God, or will we allow condemnation and legalism to control us as we depend on our emotions and obedience?

Determine that your unstable and unpredictable emotions will not dictate or deceive you. Do not allow them to be the final authority in your life. Believe what God says about you. If you're wise you will follow my example: Don't argue with the Judge.

Forsaken for Our Forgiveness

The God who created you accepts you. His Son voluntarily faced the unimaginable horror of the Cross, forsaken by God the Father and by man, in order to justify you. He was forsaken so we might be forgiven. He experienced separation so we might forever be secure in God's love. He endured the wrath of God so that we would never have to. "He was delivered over to death for our sins and was raised to life for our justification" (Ro 4:25). You have been justified!

Is it any wonder the Reformation changed Church history? There is no way to confine this doctrine. Once it is let loose it will change the life of every one it touches — including your own. ∎

GROUP DISCUSSION 1. On page 52 the author writes, "You'll never be more justified than you are at this time." What effect does this have on your efforts to live a life that pleases God?

2. Quietly meditate for a minute or two on the Cross. How

do you think Jesus felt when he realized God had forsaken him?

3. Is it possible to focus *too* much on conforming to the image of Christ?

4. What makes legalism such a subtle heresy?

5. How can we balance the doctrines of justification and sanctification without tilting toward legalism or license?

6. What one thing can we contribute to our justification? (Hint: It's nothing to brag about!)

RECOMMENDED READING

The Cross of Christ by John R. W. Stott (Downers Grove, IL: InterVarsity Press, 1986)

The Discipline of Grace by Jerry Bridges (Colorado Springs, CO: NavPress, 1994)

The Atonement by Leon Morris (Downwers Grove, IL: InterVarsity Press, 1984)

CHAPTER SIX

THE FRUITS OF JUSTIFICATION (I)

ROBIN BOISVERT

H ave you ever noticed how few Christian books have interesting covers? Oh, there are some, of course—like Franky Schaeffer's *A Time for Anger*, with its Pieter Brueghel painting of "The Blind Leading the Blind." It intrigued me to the point that I searched for the print and had it framed for my office. And then there are the delightful pictures on the jackets of C.S. Lewis' *Chronicles of Narnia* which just about transport you there.

One of the most fascinating book covers I've ever seen appeared on a series of paperback pamphlets. The illustration shows a forlorn man gazing vacantly out the barred window of a jail cell. As you look you become aware that the door to his cell is ajar behind him. But he doesn't notice. If he simply turned around he would see that he could walk out a free man. Instead he remains locked up by his own ignorance.

The point is clear enough. Many Christians—no, *most* Christians—are like this man. They are tragically unaware of the liberty and privileges which are theirs through the gospel of Jesus Christ. They are unnecessarily imprisoned saints.

Meditate on Luke 4:18-19. Do you realize this "Emancipation Proclamation" was given for you?

To change the figure only slightly, numerous slaves continued living as they always had even after the Emancipation Proclamation. Some were kept in the dark about their new standing. Others, though aware of their liberty, never walked off the plantation because of fear. Freedom requires courage and carries with it great responsibility.

It appears that the gospel has made little difference in the lives of countless Christians. Although they are truly justified and the sentence of condemnation has been lifted, the same problems seem to trouble them. The same fears, habits, and doubts that characterized their lives before they trusted Christ still hold sway. Why? I think

> **44** When God pardons, he pardons all sins, original sin and actual sin, sins of omission and of commission, secret and open sins, sins of thought, word and deed...Full pardon, or none at all, is what God designs to give. This suits human necessities. Nor is this gift ever revoked by God. When he forgives, he forgives forever.[1] **77**
>
> — **William S. Plumer**

> **44** I must take heed what I say: but the apostle saith, "God made him to be sin for us, who knew no sin, that we might be made the righteousness of God in him." Such we are in the sight of God the Father, as is the very Son of God himself. Let it be counted folly or frenzy, or fury, whatsoever, it is our comfort and our wisdom; we care for no knowledge in the world but this, that man hath sinned and God hath suffered; that God hath made himself the Son of man, and that men are made the righteousness of God.[2] **77**
>
> — **Richard Hooker**

the greatest single reason is ignorance. To not a few, the Bible is still a closed book. The fact that a tremendous inheritance has been reserved for those justified by God seems not to have dawned on them.

A growing knowledge of God's Word is vital. As you read, memorize, and meditate on the Scriptures, you will begin to experience the wonderful provision of God. The final two chapters of this book will explore the fruits of our justification, our inheritance in Christ. Any remaining doubts that may exist in your mind regarding the purpose or providence of God should be cleared as we inventory the benefits of this surpassingly great salvation.

Stepping Down from the Bench

The imagery surrounding the doctrine of justification comes straight from the law courts, as we learned in the previous chapter. God, the Lawgiver and Judge of all the earth, has issued a declaration that acquits the condemned sinner of all guilt. Justification gives us a brand-new status before God and exonerates us from all sin and the penalties associated with it. Though we were convicted felons awaiting the inevitable on Death Row, the Judge pardoned us and destroyed our criminal records. As wonderful as that is, there is an aspect of justification that is even more remarkable.

I've been in a few courtrooms and they are not very cheerful places. You can't really be yourself. It would be inappropriate to laugh out loud or put your feet up. No one thinks of getting together with the judge after the trial for ice cream or a pick-up game of basketball. There's a certain decorum to be maintained, formal and intimidating—and it's meant to be that way. This is no less true

1 Open to almost any section of your Bible and you will find wonderful promises from God. Check the one below which means the most to you right now.

❏ "Never will I leave you; never will I forsake you" (Heb 13:5).

❏ "God is faithful; he will not let you be tempted beyond what you can bear" (1Co 10:13)

❏ "Anyone who has faith in me...will do even greater things than [I do], because I am going to the Father" (Jn 14:12)

❏ "He who began a good work in you will carry it on to completion until the day of Christ Jesus" (Php 1:6)

❏ "You are no longer a slave, but a son; and since you are a son, God has made you also an heir" (Gal 4:7).

in the presence of the sovereign Judge.

But there is a monumental difference between heaven's courtroom and its earthly counterpart. For after decreeing that we are free from all accusation and condemnation, God opts *not* to retire ceremoniously to his chambers as would be expected. Instead, he violates all precedent by stepping down from the bench, gathering us into his arms, and then carrying us from the courtroom to the family room.

To have God as our Father is truly amazing. The Scriptures make it quite clear that we are legally and intimately related to God. Not only that, but to be his children carries certain privileges. Paul described it like this: "The Spirit himself testifies with our spirit that we are God's children. Now if we are children, then we are heirs—heirs of God and co-heirs with Christ" (Ro 8:17).

While justification is for us a free gift, it cost the Father his Son. It cost the Son his life. And it will cost us our pride, for the only way to receive this gift is to come before God in humility and repentant faith.

What It's All About

For Further Study:
What are the "riches" Paul describes in Colossians 2:2-3? Where do the "treasures" reside? Have you taken full advantage of this inheritance?

Children of God. Heirs of God. Co-heirs with Christ. What does it all mean? Let's first establish one crucial fact. Jesus Christ, God's only Son, is the Father's true and rightful heir. Any inheritance we have is ours only because we are "in Christ" (Eph 2:7). Furthermore, Christ himself embodies this inheritance. *He* is our peace, *he* is our righteousness, our hope, our sanctification and redemption. In *him* are hidden all the treasures of wisdom and knowledge. *He* is the resurrection and the life. The greatest thing we will ever receive from God is Jesus himself.

It's also important to understand that salvation comes not through a doctrine but through a Person. We're not saved by justification, but by Jesus. When we take time to study God's Word we run the risk of becoming expert in doctrine yet inept in the true knowledge of our Lord. And knowing him is what it's all about.

For Further Study:
How could the man who lived through the experiences recorded in 2 Corinthians 11:23-33 write Romans 15:13?

2 Read Matthew 7:21-23 and then answer the following questions:

• What praiseworthy things did these individuals accomplish?

• What is God's four-word assessment of them?

• In one sentence, how would you sum up their fatal mistake?

A friend of mine told me the following story about Scott McGregor, a dedicated Christian and an outstanding left-handed pitcher for the Baltimore Orioles in the '70s and '80s. Once, at a crucial point in a game, Scott found himself facing a dangerous hitter with men in scoring position. He was taking a good bit of time to survey the situation when an impatient woman in the box seats behind the Orioles dugout screamed out, "Jesus Christ! Pitch the ball!"

Now it's not uncommon to hear the Lord's name used in vain at a ball game. On this occasion, however, McGregor was so taken aback that he nearly lost concentration. Recovering himself, he managed to make the right pitch and the inning was over. Then he did something totally uncharacteristic, something players are not supposed to do. As he walked back to the dugout he looked directly at the lady and spoke to her. In a distressed but caring tone, full of concern for her and his Lord, he said, "Lady, if you really knew Him, you'd *never* say his name like that."

McGregor demonstrated that Christianity is more than a truth to be believed. It's a life to be lived and, most of all, a Lord to be loved.

When considering something as vast and wonderful as the inheritance we have in Christ, described by Paul as "the incomparable riches of his grace" (Eph 2:7), it's hard to know where to begin. Interestingly, Paul had a similar problem. In his letter to the Ephesians, he gets carried away with the overwhelming implications of justification. As he attempts in the first chapter to relate all that God has done and is doing, he begins a sentence in verse three that doesn't end until eleven verses later. It may not be grammatically pretty, but his overflowing heart bears testimony to the unfathomable grace of God.

The following passage from Paul's epistle to the Romans provides an excellent starting point: "Therefore, since we have been justified through faith, we have peace with God through our Lord Jesus Christ, through whom we have gained access by faith into this grace in which we now stand. And we rejoice in the hope of the glory of God" (Ro 5:1-2). John Stott explains the significance of this passage:

The earlier chapters of [Romans] are devoted to the need and the way of justification. They are concerned to make it plain that all men are sinners under the just judgment of God, and can be justified solely through the redemption which is in Christ Jesus—by grace alone, through faith alone. Now, at this point, having set forth the need and explained the way of justification, Paul goes on to describe its *fruits,* the *results of justification* in a life of sonship and obedience on earth and a glorious hereafter in heaven (emphasis added).[3]

This chapter will look at three of justification's fruits: peace with God (reconciliation), forgiveness of sins, and the process of sanctification. In the final chapter of this book we will examine our adoption in Christ as well as our hope of future glory.

Peace with God

Peace with God underlies everything else we receive in Christ. It is the gift that puts all other blessings in perspective. "The primary business of the Christian gospel is not to give us blessings," writes D. Martyn Lloyd-Jones. "Its primary purpose is to reconcile us to God."[4] Having peace with God means we are in a state of reconciliation with him. The declaration of justification has removed all obstacles between God and man. While there is certainly a subjective peace *of* God (that is, one that can be felt), what Paul has in mind in Romans 5:1 is the *objective* fact that the gospel has removed everything that divided us from God.

To reconcile means to bring together those who had been separated because of hostility. A prime example of this meaning is found in Stephen's speech to the Sanhedrin when he recounts an incident from the life of Moses: "The next day Moses came upon two Israelites who were fighting. He tried to *reconcile* them by saying, 'Men, you are brothers; why do you want to hurt each other?'" (Ac 7:26). The King James version of the Bible translates "reconcile" in this context as "set them at one again." The Greek word used is the verb form of the word normally translated "peace." What's important for us to keep in mind is that now, from God's point of view, there is no more hostility between God and those who are justified. His anger and wrath against sin were justly expressed and fully satisfied at the Cross. The battle is over. Peace has been made.

Meditate on Ephesians 2:11-20.
What did Jesus do to the barrier of hostility that stood between himself and us?

Not only has the conflict been resolved, but any legal problems resulting from former hostilities have been erased, never to reappear: "Therefore, there is now no condemnation for those who are in Christ Jesus...Who will bring any charge against those whom God has chosen? It is God who justifies" (Ro 8:1,33). If the highest tribunal in the universe has declared us justified, there is not a charge that can stick.

Be aware that the phrase "no condemnation" does *not* mean "no accusation." We touched on that in the first chapter. The enemy of our souls continues his dirty work of casting aspersions and shooting fiery darts, and it often happens that we mistake God's gifts of conviction and correction for the devil's denunciation. But the fact that Jesus has taken our place means we shall never have to face the condemnation of final judgment. "Who is he that condemns? Christ Jesus, who died—more than that, who was raised to life—is at the right hand of God and is also interceding for us" (Ro 8:34). The only One authorized to condemn for eternity has instead ruled in our favor.

Knowing that we have peace with God puts our minds at rest. It enables us to overcome worries and fears. Even if the entire world were to oppose us, we are secure in Christ. "Do not be afraid of those who kill the body and after that can do no more," Jesus explained to his disciples, who were destined to face great opposition. "But I will show you whom you should fear: Fear him who, after the killing of the body, has power to throw you into hell" (Lk 12:4,5). God, the One worthy of our fear, has initiated an eternal pact of peace with us. For the Christian who is established in this truth, even the fear of death is vanquished because the threat of judgment no longer exists.

> ❝ When our holy war with God ceases, when we like Luther walk through the doors of Paradise, when we are justified by faith, the war ends forever. With the cleansing from sin and the declaration of divine forgiveness we enter into a peace treaty with God that is eternal. The firstfruit of our justification is peace with God. This peace is a holy peace, a peace unblemished and transcendent. It is a peace that cannot be destroyed.[5] ❞
>
> — R.C. Sproul

3 Imagine yourself ruling over a nation of five billion people. Word reaches you that a citizen has staged a one-man coup and is rampaging across the palace grounds. Instead of sending your armored tank division to stop the madman, you send the Prince. In the act of reaching out to the rebel, the Prince is murdered. How would you treat this citizen once he is captured?

❑ Banish him forever from your kingdom

❑ Roast him slowly over an open fire

❑ Hang him from the highest tree in the city

❑ Sentence him to life in solitary confinement

❑ Feed him to the royal boa constrictor

❑ Forgive him, embrace him, and adopt him as your son

Forgiveness of Sins

Closely related to reconciliation and peace with God is the forgiveness of sins. I may be overreacting, but it seems to me this precious truth is in danger of being despised. When people lament, "I know I'm forgiven, but…," I can't help thinking, *You do* not *know you're forgiven! If you really understood forgiveness your problem wouldn't seem anywhere near as bad.* As Lloyd-Jones implies in his statement on page 63, man's greatest need is forgiveness. And if God has forgiven us, any other problem we have must be minor by comparison.

It is rare today to hear Christians rejoice in being forgiven by God. This is understandable in a culture that views low self-esteem as a greater problem than alienation from God. Yet our awareness of forgiveness directly affects our affection for God. That was the gist of our Lord's response to self-righteous Simon the Pharisee. "He who has been forgiven little loves little," Jesus told him (Lk 7:47). Conversely, those who have been forgiven much— or at least realize how much they have been forgiven— love much. Every one of us should be in that category.

Consider the following:

■ Pardon for sin comes to us only on the basis of the shed blood of Jesus Christ. "In him we have redemption through his blood, the forgiveness of sins, in accordance with the riches of God's grace" (Eph 1:7).

■ God's motive for forgiveness is his great love. His forgiveness is a free and merciful work. "God exalted him to his own right hand as Prince and Savior that he might give repentance and forgiveness of sins to Israel" (Ac 5:31)—and to Gentiles as well.

■ Forgiveness of sins leads to a knowledge of salvation. Jesus came "to give his people the knowledge of salvation through the forgiveness of their sins" (Lk 1:77).

■ Understanding forgiveness leads to a right fear of God. "If you, O Lord, kept a record of sins, O Lord, who could stand? But with you there is forgiveness; therefore you are feared" (Ps 130:3-4).

■ God's forgiveness is thorough. "I, even I, am he who blots out your transgressions, for my own sake, and remembers your sins no more" (Isa 43:25).

Meditate on Exodus 34:5-7. In light of all God's character qualities, do you find it significant that he chose to emphasize these traits when revealing himself to Moses?

4 Do any of these nagging doubts cause you to question God's forgiveness? (Check all that apply)

❑ God can't keep forgiving me over and over for the same sin.

❑ I may be forgiven, but God hasn't forgotten.

❑ Nothing is free in life—God must expect some type of repayment.

❑ I'm guilty of the unforgivable sin.

❑ After sin #491 God will reject me (see Mt 18:22).

❑ Other _____

The following story, recounted by Becky Pippert in her book *Hope Has Its Reasons,* shows the power of forgiveness in one woman's life. It's worth quoting at length:

"Several years ago after I had finished speaking at a conference, a lovely woman came to the platform. She obviously wanted to speak to me and the moment I turned to her, tears welled up in her eyes. We made our way to a room where we could talk privately. It was clear from looking at her that she was sensitive but tortured. She sobbed as she told me the following story.

"Years before, she and her fiance (to whom she was now married) had been the youth workers at a large conservative church. They were a well-known couple and had an extraordinary impact on the young people. Everyone looked up to them and admired them tremendously. A few months before they were to be married they began having sexual relations. That left them burdened enough with a sense of guilt and hypocrisy. But then she discovered she was pregnant. 'You can't imagine what the implications would have been of admitting this to our church,' she said. 'To confess that we were preaching one thing and living another would have been intolerable. The congregation was so conservative and had never been touched by any scandal. We felt they wouldn't be able to handle knowing about our situation. Nor could we bear the humiliation.

'So we made the most excruciating decision I have ever made. I had an abortion. My wedding day was the worst day of my entire life. Everyone in the church was smiling at me, thinking me a bride beaming in innocence. But do you know what was going through my head as I walked down the aisle? All I could think to myself was, 'You're a murderer. You were so proud that you couldn't bear the shame and humiliation of being exposed for what you are. But I know what you are and so does God. You have murdered an innocent baby.'

"She was sobbing so deeply that she could not speak. As I put my arms around her a thought came to me very strongly. But I was afraid to say it. I knew if it was not from God that it could be very destructive. So I prayed silently for the wisdom to help her.

"She continued. 'I just can't believe that I could do something so horrible. How could I have murdered an

> **❝** In relationship both to sin and to God, the determining factor of my existence is *no longer my past.* It is *Christ's* past.[6] **❞**
>
> — **Sinclair Ferguson**

For Further Study:
Read Isaiah 59. How does God respond to our appalling lack of righteousness? (See verses 16 and 20)

innocent life? How is it possible I could do such a thing? I love my husband, we have four beautiful children. I know the Bible says that God forgives all of our sins. But I can't forgive myself! I've confessed this sin a thousand times and I still feel such shame and sorrow. The thought that haunts me the most is *how* could I murder an innocent life?'

"I took a deep breath and said what I had been thinking. 'I don't know why you are so surprised. This isn't the first time your sin has led to death, it's the second.' She looked at me in utter amazement. 'My dear friend,' I continued, 'when you look at the Cross, all of us show up as crucifiers. Religious or nonreligious, good or bad, aborters or nonaborters—all of us are responsible for the death of the only innocent who ever lived. Jesus died for all of our sins—past, present, and future. Do you think there are any sins of yours that Jesus didn't have to die for? The very sin of pride that caused you to destroy your child is what killed Christ as well. It does not matter that you weren't there two thousand years ago. We all sent him there. Luther said that we carry his very nails in our pockets. So if you have done it before, then why couldn't you do it again?'

"She stopped crying. She looked me straight in the eyes and said, 'You're absolutely right. I have done something even worse than killing my baby. My sin is what drove Jesus to the Cross. It doesn't matter that I wasn't there pounding in the nails, I'm still responsible for his death. Do you realize the significance of what you are telling me, Becky? I came to you saying I had done the worst thing imaginable. And you tell me I have done something even worse than that.'

"I grimaced because I knew this was true. (I am not sure that my approach would qualify as one of the great counseling techniques!) Then she said, 'But, Becky, if the Cross shows me that I am far worse than I had ever imagined, it also shows me that my evil has been absorbed and forgiven. If the worst thing any human can do is to kill God's son, and *that* can be forgiven, then how can anything else—even my abortion—not be forgiven?'

"I will never forget the look in her eyes as she sat back in awe and quietly said, 'Talk about amazing grace.' This time she wept not out of sorrow but

---

Meditate on Psalm 32:1-5. What happens when we keep our sins hidden? What happens when we confess them?

---

5 Do you find yourself burdened by guilt when you remember a specific sin (or sins) from the past? If so, seek out a mature Christian to whom you can confess and from whom you can receive encouragement about the extent of God's forgiveness. Put your intention in writing:

"Believing that God wants to release me

from guilt, I will talk to_____

about this area of sin no later than _____

_____."

from relief and gratitude. I saw a woman literally transformed by a proper understanding of the Cross."[7]

Forgiveness of sins is a critical concern. The greatest of the English Puritan theologians, John Owen, wrote a treatise on the subject that still stands as a classic. This exposition of Psalm 130 is over three hundred pages long, although the psalm itself has only eight verses. The editor's preface yields some insight into the circumstances surrounding the work. It seems that as a young man Owen had only a superficial awareness of God's forgiveness, "until the Lord was pleased to visit me with a sore affliction, whereby I was brought to the mouth of the grave, and under which my soul was oppressed with horror and darkness; but God graciously relieved my spirit by a powerful application of Psalm 130:4 from whence I received special instruction, peace and comfort, in drawing near to God through the Mediator, and preached thereupon immediately after my recovery."[9]

> **"** When once you realize all that it cost God to forgive you, you will be held as in a vice, constrained by the love of God.[8] **"**
> — Oswald Chambers

Psalm 130:4, as we saw above, shows that fearing the Lord is the natural outgrowth of embracing his forgiveness. While we're young and healthy other problems can seem so much more important. But when our eyes are opened to the affairs of eternity, knowing whether or not we are truly forgiven will make all other matters pale into insignificance.

Sanctification through Christ

Justification sets in motion the process called sanctification, by which we become more and more like Jesus. While justification leaves us forgiven and loved, it does nothing for our character. We're still the same rascals we were before God saved us. It would be tragic if God were to leave us to ourselves. We would never grow, never change, never improve. Fortunately, although God loves us as we are, he loves us too much to leave us there.

Central to the doctrine of sanctification is the truth that we are united with Jesus Christ. In his book *Men Made New,* John Stott makes the following observation:

The great theme of Romans 6, and in particular of verses 1-11, is that the death and resurrection of Jesus Christ are not only historical facts and significant doctrines, but personal experiences of the Christian believer. They are events in which we ourselves have come to share. All Christians have been united to Christ in his death and resurrection. Further, if this is true, if we have died with Christ and risen with Christ, it is inconceivable that we should go on living in sin."[10]

Perhaps you did a double-take when you hit that word "inconceivable." Most of us find it inconceivable that we could possibly go on living *outside* of sin! Is victory over sin actually possible?

For Further Study:
Read 1 Corinthians 15:51-58. Though this passage refers to the future, how can this truth strengthen you in your present battle against sin?

Here are two common answers. Some say Christians can expect a life of victory in the hereafter, but should set their sights low in the here and now. Others have had such dramatic deliverances from gross sin that they consider themselves practically immune to it. Both these extremes are way off target. While applying the lesson will require some spiritual effort, we have in the sixth chapter of Romans all the teaching we need to set us straight.

"What shall we say, then?" Paul asks (v.1). "Shall we go on sinning so that grace may increase?" He anticipates this question because a few verses earlier he said, "But where sin increased, grace increased all the more" (Ro 5:20). He knew that statement would lead some to reason as follows: "If God is glorified in forgiving sin and if grace increases in proportion to sin, why not sin all the more? Then there will be more grace and God will receive more glory!" What a self-serving and warped inference. That Paul even stated the matter this way indicates that his gospel had been subject to abuse. It's worth noting, however, that Paul did not retract or reword the doctrine. If the gospel is rightly preached it will always be vulnerable to this misinterpretation.

Paul powerfully refutes his own suggestion that grace leads to further sin: "May it never be! Seeing that we have died to sin, how shall we still live in it?" (Ro 6:2, Cranfield's translation). Our death to sin, as Paul explains in the following verses, is wrapped up in our union with a crucified Christ. When we believed on Jesus, we became united with him. A faith transaction occurred in which we were forever to be counted as "in Christ," that is, spiritually joined to

> **❝** In justification our own works have no place at all and simple faith in Christ is the one thing needful. In sanctification our own works are of vast importance, and God bids us fight and watch and pray and strive and take pains and labour.[11] **❞**
>
> — **J.C. Ryle**

6 After reading this chapter, a young but sincere Christian comes to you for help. "Paul says my old self has died and is buried with Christ," she says. "So why does it feel so alive every time my ex-boyfriend drops by?" How would you answer?

❏ "You must have a demon—let's cast it out!"

❏ "I guess you weren't really saved after all."

❏ "Where's your faith, sister?"

❏ "Maybe your old self was just in a temporary coma."

❏ "Let's look at the sixth and seventh chapters of Romans..."

Meditate on Romans 6:17-18. We're no longer slaves to sin, but we're still slaves. To what has your new master called you?

him. This union is symbolized by baptism. As Jesus died, was buried, and rose to live a new, empowered life, so we also died with him, were buried with him by baptism, and are raised up to live a new life in a new way.

The closest natural analogy of this union is marriage. My wife Clara and I have a shared identity (we both have the same last name) and are united in heart, mind, and body. We share our resources—everything I have is hers, and vice versa. As a result we are both enriched (though here's where the analogy is weak—we gain a one-sided benefit in our union with Christ). Clara and I wear rings that symbolize the deeper truth of our oneness. But just as my ring doesn't make me married, so baptism doesn't make me a Christian. It comes after the fact of the faith transaction.

What exactly does it mean to be dead to sin? I'm dead to sin in the sense that the guilt and penalty attached to sin (death) are no longer hanging over me. But beyond that, my relationship with sin has been radically changed. Before I was justified, I couldn't help sinning. Now I am no longer under sin's dominion. *The master-slave relationship that once existed has been forever ended.* Notice the language employed in Romans 6:12-14: "Do not let sin reign...Do not offer the parts of your body to sin...Sin shall not be your master." This is the language of slavery and Paul says it no longer applies. Our obligation to sin has been ended—by death.

Our death to sin through our union with Christ has far-reaching implications. Any problems or habits or memories or hang-ups that currently influence your thoughts and behavior need not do so any longer. They can be successfully resisted. The person who was once dominated by them—your old self—has died. These sinful impulses are no longer your master.

Long before anyone popularized the claim that there are only two kinds of people in the world (for example, those who live in Oshkosh, Wisconsin and those who *wish* they lived there), John

> ❝ It's not that I'm not able to sin, but that I'm able not to sin. ❞
>
> — **Arthur Wallis**

Owen made his own classification. He distinguished between those who were under the dominion of sin and those who *thought* they were under its dominion. A pastor consequently had two primary responsibilities, as Owen expressed it in the language of his day:

> 1. To convince those in whom sin evidently hath the dominion that such indeed is their state and condition.
>
> 2. To satisfy some that sin hath not the dominion over them, notwithstanding its restless acting itself in them and warring against their souls; yet unless this can be done, it is impossible they should enjoy solid peace and comfort in this life.[12]

It has been my privilege more than once to see people overcome longstanding problems and defiling habits through the diligent study and application of Romans 6. We need not remain imprisoned saints any longer. Once we become aware that we have been united with Christ in his death and resurrection, we'll see he has opened wide the door of our deliverance. ■

GROUP DISCUSSION 1. Think back to the opening illustration of the imprisoned saint. What does the jail symbolize? What is the key?

2. What inner conflict could have possibly held a slave back from responding to Lincoln's Emancipation Proclamation? What could hold back a Christian from seizing his liberty in Christ?

3. What's the greatest thing we will ever receive from God? (Page 61)

4. What emotions do you think Americans experienced when peace was announced at the end of World War II? Does your peace with God evoke similar emotions in you?

5. According to the author, what is man's greatest need?

6. Read the story of Simon the Pharisee and the sinful woman in Luke 7:36-50. What's the main difference between these two? With which of them do you identify most in your attitude toward Jesus?

7. Were you affected by the story about the woman who had an abortion? How?

8. What attitudes or actions might indicate that someone has a superficial awareness of forgiveness?

9. What does it mean to be united with Christ in his death? What are the implications?

RECOMMENDED READING

Men Made New by John R.W. Stott (Grand Rapids, MI: Baker Book House, 1966)

The Atonement by Leon Morris (Downwers Grove, IL: InterVarsity Press, 1984)

The Glory of Christ by Peter Lewis (Chicago, IL: Moody Press, 1997)

CHAPTER SEVEN

THE FRUITS OF JUSTIFICATION (II)

ROBIN BOISVERT

I n the last chapter we touched briefly on the special relationship we now enjoy. I'm speaking of the fact that God has become our Father. Remember our friend looking sadly out of his unlocked jail cell? If he would only turn around he would see more than just an open door. He'd see a Father waiting to receive him.

I can vividly recall one Saturday morning with my father. The two of us were sitting at the kitchen table when the phone rang. I was a young man at the time and far from God. As I answered the phone, my heart sank. The caller identified himself as a detective with the Montgomery County Police Department, Glenmont Station. Using police-speak terms, he informed me that I had been observed using a controlled substance (marijuana) at a particular residence the evening before (which was true). I was placed under arrest and instructed to turn myself in.

My father could tell from my expression that something was very wrong. "What's the matter?!" he asked.

I could only respond vacantly, "I'm busted."

What followed was uproarious laughter from the other end of the line. I had been set up by some "friends" of mine. The law-breaking fool was also a gullible fool. It hadn't occurred to me that the police don't arrest people over the telephone. As a courtesy, they do it in person.

While I'll never forget that practical joke, what made much more of an impression on me was Dad's response. He could have yelled at me for being the disgrace I certainly was. Instead, his first move was to affirm his love and support for me. That affected me deeply. I have no doubt Dad would have taken my place and my punishment, if possible. His loyalty was the opposite of what I deserved.

Jesus told a story of another foolish son who, after selfishly and prematurely demanding his share of the family inheritance, proceeded to squander it. When finally he ran out of resources, the prodigal son decided to return home to his father and ask for the opportunity, not to be restored as a son, but to hire on as a servant. "Father, I have sinned against heaven and against you. I am no longer worthy to be called your son; make me like one of your hired men" (Lk 15:18-19). The father had every right to ridicule and reject the son; even accepting him as a laborer would have been a sign of real generosity. Instead, he watched eagerly for his return, and welcomed his son with gifts and a feast. God's mercy is displayed in this story as the father showers his boy with love, forgiveness, and acceptance—not at all what the son expected or deserved.

Meditate on John 8:1-11. What penalty did this woman deserve for her sin? What did she receive?

Thus far our study of justification has yielded undeniable evidence that this is indeed a great salvation. We have learned how to combat the persistent influence of accusation and adversity. We've navigated the sobering subjects of our own sin, of God's holiness and wrath. We've taken a close-up look at the Cross, where our Savior suffered the condemnation we deserved so that we might be justified before God. There he obtained for us peace with the One who had been the object of our hostility; forgiveness from the One against whom we had sinned; and a union with himself that empowers us in our striving against evil.

Now we conclude with a look at two final aspects of our inheritance in Christ: adoption and the hope of future glory.

Revealing the Father

Biblical theology teaches us to expect an unfolding, progressive revelation in Scripture.[1] For example, the mysterious message in Genesis 3 about a woman's seed bruising a serpent's head becomes open and apparent in the New Testament declaration of Jesus' crucifixion and subsequent resurrection. Similarly, the Old Testament gives us only the broadest outlines of what is a central revelation in the New Testament: the fatherhood of God. To be sure, there are passages that speak of Israel as the firstborn son of God as well as other snippets of this truth. But even then the idea is usually meant in a nationalistic sense. He's the Father of Israel, not of individuals. For the

> **❝** How great is the love the Father has lavished on us, that we should be called children of God! And that is what we are! The reason the world does not know us is that it did not know him. Dear friends, now we are children of God, and what we will be has not yet been made known. But we know that when he appears, we shall be like him, for we shall see him as he is. **❞**
>
> — John the Apostle

most part, the Old Testament portrays God not as our Father, but as an awesome and holy King.

Of course, God has always been Father, and Jesus Christ has always been God the Son. But it was necessary for Jesus to come and reveal God as Father to us because, as John explains in his Gospel, he was the only one qualified to do so: "No one has ever seen God, but God the One and Only, who is at the Father's side, has made him known" (Jn 1:18).

In this verse, the Greek for "made him known" is the word from which we get "exegesis." "Exegesis" means to explain or to rehearse the facts about something. For instance, to exegete a passage of Scripture is to teach it in such a way as to unfold its meaning. Jesus, who is at the Father's side, a place of intimacy and tenderness, is perfectly positioned to know the Father completely. And an important part of Jesus' ministry is to make him known to us. He imparted that truth effectively to his disciples, and the gospels continue to impart it to us today.

Meditate on John 17:25-26. What was Jesus' purpose in making the Father known?

Each time Jesus referred to God as his Father, he was making what at that time was a revolutionary claim. Not everybody appreciated it. The Pharisees in particular resented Jesus because by speaking of God as his Father he implied he was equal to God. But the verse above makes it clear that Jesus had the right to "exegete" the Father. Indeed, it would have been impossible for him not to have done so. Because he was of the same essence as the Father and the Spirit, Jesus shed light on God's identity as he revealed himself.

This last point warrants a brief tangent. What is the relationship between God the Father and God the Son? Augustine, the most influential theologian of the early Church, classifies Scripture's teaching on the nature of this relationship into three groups:

1 Your church feels directed to reach out to a remote island tribe in the South Pacific. Because you're the only one who speaks the Polynesian dialect, you find yourself parachuting into a clearing surrounded by expectant villagers. What are the first five attributes of God (for example, his power or kindness) that you would "exegete" for this tribe?

• _____

• _____

• _____

• _____

• _____

■ Those verses which reveal that Jesus is inferior to his Father because of his incarnation. He willingly set aside his glory (Php 2:5-8) and was born as a baby. Consequently he experienced hunger, thirst, fatigue, and other weaknesses his Father has never known. In this human condition Jesus knew his Father was greater, and he willingly sought and submitted to his Father's guidance. We find one clear example of this in the Garden of Gethsemane: "Going a little farther, [Jesus] fell with his face to the ground and prayed, 'My Father, if it is possible, may this cup be taken from me. Yet not as I will, but as you will'" (Mt 26:39).

■ Those verses which teach that Jesus, from before the foundation of the world, was with the Father yet distinct from him. "In the beginning was the Word, and the Word was with God, and the Word was God" (Jn 1:1). "But you, Bethlehem Ephrathah, though you are small among the clans of Judah, out of you will come for me one who will be ruler over Israel, whose origins are from of old, from ancient times" (Mic 5:2).

■ Those verses which show that the Father and Son are not separate Gods, but are of one essence. "I and the Father are one" (Jn 10:30).[2]

For Further Study:
Read Deuteronomy 6:4 and you'll understand why the Pharisees accused Jesus of blasphemy when he claimed God was his father. What verses can you find in the New Testament that shed light on the Trinity?

Do you want to know the Father? Look at Jesus. On the evening of the last supper, Philip asked, "Lord, show us the Father and we shall be satisfied." Jesus replied, "Anyone who has seen me *has* seen the Father" (Jn 14:8-9 RSV, emphasis added). Do you want to know the Father's ways? Look at Jesus. "I tell you the truth, the Son can do nothing by himself; he can do only what he sees his Father doing, because whatever the Father does the Son also does" (Jn 5:19). Do you want to increase in the knowledge of the Father? Look at Jesus. "The Son is the radiance of God's glory and the exact representation of his being" (Heb 1:3).

Jesus redefined our relationship with God. In a private moment with his disciples shortly before his death, Jesus said, "I no longer call you servants, because a servant does not know his master's business. Instead, I have called you friends, for everything that I learned from my Father I have made known to you" (Jn 15:15). Through the teaching of the Law the Jewish people learned to revere a stern and distant Master. Through the life and death of Jesus we have been reconciled to a loving and intimate Father.

Adoption: Our Antidote to Angst

This unique relationship between God and all who have been justified is explained in the doctrine of adoption, also referred to as "sonship." It points out our status as children of God and refers to the means by which we become his children. Adoption into God's family takes place not by birth, but by rebirth. It occurs not by maturation, but by regeneration. It's not natural, but supernatural.[4]

> What is a Christian? The question can be answered in many ways, but the richest answer I know is that a Christian is one who has God for his Father.[3]
>
> — J.I. Packer

Adoption is a gift of grace which becomes ours through receiving Jesus Christ. "To all who received him, to those who believed in his name, he gave the right to become children of God" (Jn 1:12). Note the condition here. God is not the universal father of all humanity. That's a presumptuous and humanistic notion. God is *creator* of all, but he is the Father only of those who have received Christ.

The term "adoption" is used in the Bible exclusively by Paul. Growing up as he did in Tarsus, he would have been familiar with the custom as it existed in the Roman Empire. Adoption then was different from our present conception of it in at least two significant ways. First, the Greeks and Romans adopted adults, not infants. Rather than being given up for adoption, an unwanted baby (more often than not a female) was typically cast out and left to die from exposure. Correspondence of the day reflects this heartless practice in a chillingly matter-of-fact tone.

Second, because this was primarily a legal arrangement, adoption in the Gentile world did not carry the warmth and selfless love which we associate it with today. It was pragmatic—a business transaction. If someone lacked an heir, he would adopt a male of legal age to carry on the family heritage and estate. Adoption served as a form of social security. According to one commentator, "The adoptive son entered at once into the rights of the parent and undertook out of the assigned income to keep the testator and his family to the end of their lives...Hence adoption was a way of providing for old age."[5]

Though Paul was undoubtedly aware of Roman-style adoption, it is more than likely that his knowledge of the Old Testament and Jewish history shaped his perspective on adoption. Although the word "adoption" never occurs in the Old Testament, the concept certainly does. And it is here that the kindness, joy, and sacrificial love which we (together with Paul) attach to adoption is found. William Hendriksen writes, "How completely different (from the Roman model) is the nature of adoption as practiced in the Old Testament...Did not Pharaoh's daughter 'adopt' Moses (Ex 2:10), even though he was only, humanly speaking, a helpless child? Did not Mordecai bring up his cousin, *a girl* named Esther (Est 2:7)?"[6]

Paul's writings frequently employ terms from everyday language and invest them with deeper spiritual meaning. Hendriksen suggests that his reference to adoption follows that pattern: "When in Romans 8:15 and Galatians 4:5 Paul uses the term "adoption," the *word* and the *legal standing* were borrowed from Roman practice, but the *essence* from the divine revelation in the Old Testament."[7]

Adoption touches a profound human need, a universal insecurity. The New Testament speaks of "those who all their lives were held in slavery by their fear of death" (Heb 2:15). Of course, many claim to be unafraid. But the entire human race struggles under what a German philosopher of the twentieth century has called "angst," a nagging anxiety lurking just below the surface of the soul. This is not an anxiety that can be traced to any specific cause. It is vague and shadowy—but very real. Some have described this anxiety as the feeling of being hurled into a brutal and incomprehensible existence, or of being abandoned by one's parents.

Salvation through Jesus Christ is the only answer to this fear. "For you did not receive a spirit that makes you a slave again to fear," wrote Paul, "but you received the Spirit of sonship [adoption]. And by him we cry, 'Abba, Father'" (Ro 8:15). Perhaps the only way to capture the vivid imagery of this verse is with a true story.

I have a friend who adopted a child in Seoul, Korea. He describes how difficult it was to stand amidst that crowd of needy, unwanted children at the orphanage. They all hungered for attention, and pressed against him in hopes of receiving a touch or a smile. Seeing their desperate little faces

Meditate on John 14:1-4. Far from abandoning you to a meaningless existence, God is arranging eternal accommodations just for you—and luxury accommodations at that!

> **❝** [Adoption] bestows upon its recipients not only a new name, a new legal standing, and a new family-relationship, but also a new image, the image of Christ (Ro 8:29). Earthly parents may love an adopted child ever so much. Nevertheless, they are, to a certain extent, unable to impart their spirit to that child; but when God adopts, he imparts to us the Spirit of his Son.[8] **❞**
>
> **— William Hendriksen**

made him want to take them all. Yet as painful as it was to turn the others away, he recalls that joyful moment when he singled out his soon-to-be daughter Renee and took her in his arms.

Now, whenever Renee struggles with typical childish insecurities, all she has to do is ask, "Dad, do you really love me?" Because she was adopted, her father can answer her in a unique way. "Renee," he can say, "you weren't forced on me. I didn't have to bring you into my family. I wasn't under any compulsion. But I *wanted* to, Renee. I wanted you so much that I traveled half way around the world to find you just so that I could make you my daughter. I deliberately chose you, Renee, and I will always, always love you."

Jesus didn't have to leave heaven and come to earth. He wasn't under compulsion. Why did he come? So that he could look you in the eye and say, "You! I'll take *you!* No longer will you be alienated, no longer will you be my enemy. I'm going to change you. I'm going to be reconciled to you. *You will be my child!"*

To insure that we grasp the full implications of adoption, Paul uses the Aramaic word "Abba." It's an informal term resident in the vocabulary of any toddler—we would translate it "Daddy." This is how Jesus addressed God as he sweated drops of blood in Gethsemane's garden. He didn't approach his Father with the stiff, courteous tone of voice you might expect from an English schoolboy. In his passion he prayed, *"Abba! Daddy!"* Paul says adoption evokes a *cry* from our hearts, a very strong word. And listen to Martin Luther's sixteenth-century remarks about this phrase:

> This is but a little word, and yet notwithstanding it comprehendeth all things. The mouth speaketh not, but the affection of the heart speaketh after this manner. Although I be oppressed with anguish and terror on every side, and seem to be forsaken and utterly cast away from thy presence, yet am I thy child, and thou art my Father for Christ's sake: I am beloved because of the Beloved. Wherefore this little

2 Under the proper headings below, briefly describe three things about a child's life that change with human adoption, then note the corresponding changes that occur with divine adoption.

Human Adoption	Divine Adoption
•	•
•	•
•	•

word, Father, conceived effectually in the heart, pas-
seth all the eloquence of Demosthenes, Cicero, and
of the most eloquent rhetoricians that ever were in
the world. This matter is not expressed with words,
but with groanings, which groanings cannot be
uttered with any words of eloquence, for no tongue
can express them.[9]

For Further Study:
According to Galatians
4:1-7, even though we
were heirs to a rich
estate, something had
to take place before we
could gain our inheri-
tance. What was it?

The word "Abba" indicates freedom, confidence, joyful
recognition, sweet response, overwhelming gratitude, and
filial trust.[10] In this word we find our antidote to angst.
The Spirit we have received, far from producing fear and
bondage, has set us free to call upon God in the most intimate way possible.

My favorite part of the day occurs when I arrive at
home after work to the delight of my four children, who
repeatedly shout "Daddy! Daddy!" as they shower me with
hugs and kisses. As uncomplicated and informal as this
greeting is to them, it is wonderful and fulfilling to me. I
don't doubt that our cries affect our heavenly Father in a
similar way.

Feeling the Father's Care

At more than one point in this book we have seen that
justification is an objective reality unaffected by the shift-
ing state of our emotions. Feelings make a poor foundation for our fellowship with God, and emotionalism is
often counter-productive. But to argue against feelings
and define the faith solely in terms of act and fact is to cut
the heart out of God's love. If emotions are so easily rec-
ognized and appreciated in human relationships, why
would we eliminate them from our relationship with God?

There is a subjective element to knowing God, and it's
this to which Paul refers in Romans 8:16: "The Spirit himself testifies with our spirit that we are God's children."
The inward sense of God's presence, the emotional awareness of his loving Spirit is an important fruit (though not
a root) of justification. To believe otherwise is sub-
Christian.

One of the Holy Spirit's most important functions is to
bless us with the assurance that we are indeed God's children. As philosopher Blaise Pascal once said, "The heart
has its reasons, that reason knows nothing of."[11]

I don't mean to imply that one must become a mystic
to enjoy the feeling of God's love. As a matter of fact, the
more knowledge we acquire regarding Scripture's claims

3 Any tree that mistakes its fruits for its roots will have a hard time growing. That's true for Christians as well. With the help of the following diagram, identify five roots (from Romans 8: 29-30, see pages 3-4 for a reminder) and nine fruits (from Galatians 5:22) of the Christian life.

about God's fatherhood, the more we will be aware of his continual presence.

The fact that we are included in God's family at all is a marvelous thing, though at first glance that may not be apparent. After all, most of us grew up in families and took them for granted. We probably failed to adequately appreciate the extent of Mom's sacrificial love and Dad's provision. Gratitude does not come automatically. The sad part is that if we don't learn to be thankful for these blessings, we grow to expect them as our due. In the same way we can take our Father's goodness for granted. Here we are, orphans transplanted from the filthiest alleys into the King's own palace, and still our tendency is to gripe and complain. How fortunate we are to have a Father whose love is surpassed only by his patience.

A brief excursion into a few of our Father's many ways of caring for us can help us appreciate his love more fully. To begin with, let's not overlook his providential care. We all know he causes rain to fall on the unjust as well as the just, but that doesn't make it any less wonderful. Stop and think of all the "mundane" things we take for granted like food, shelter, family, and friends. These are no less gracious gifts from a loving Father than are prophecy and words of knowledge.

The language is a bit archaic, but Sir Robert Grant captures the wonder of our Father's providence in his hymn, *O Worship the King:*

Thy bountiful care, what tongue can recite?

Meditate on Psalm 145:15-16. Take a moment to thank God for the way he has opened his hand for you.

It breathes in the air, it shines in the light.
It streams from the hills, it descends to the plain,
And sweetly distills in the dew and the rain.

These manifestations of our Father's tender consideration are well-deserving of poetry. And thinking of such benefits has the added advantage of putting us squarely in our place! There is no room for pride when we see how dependent we are on our Father's providential provision.

> **"** To be right with God the judge is a great thing, but to be loved and cared for by God the father is a greater.[12] **"**
>
> — J.I. Packer

The English are a people of many titles. Lords and ladies, dukes and earls abound. One very interesting title is "Lord Protector." King Edward was only a boy when he inherited the throne from his father, Henry VIII, so it fell to the Lord Protector to oversee the young king as well as the kingdom's affairs. God is our Lord Protector. He takes charge of our affairs for our good and effectively shields us from danger.

I'm a rather mild-mannered person by nature, not at all given to temper (except on the golf course). But I've noticed a certain courage or righteous anger that rises up in me when anything threatens my wife and children. It seems almost instinctive. I believe God put it there, and while I'm sure it could be expressed sinfully, it need not— it's for the protection of my family. Having a protective heavenly Father enables us to relax in childlike trust, just as my human father served as a refuge for me during a difficult experience several years ago.

My wife's first pregnancy ended in miscarriage. It was a very sorrowful time. But neither of us were prepared for the danger that followed. Because we lost the baby in the middle of the night, the doctor instructed us to come to the hospital first thing in the morning. Clara bled profusely, but we assumed that to be normal...until 6:00 a.m., that is, when she passed out and went into shock. I struggled to call the ambulance and care for her at the same time. Though it was touch and go for a while, we finally got her to the hospital where her condition stabilized. What a relief!

Part of a pastor's job is to manage responsibly in times of crisis, so as I handled admittance forms and other details throughout the morning I kept my emotions in check. Then it was time to make phone calls to let others

For Further Study:
For an intimate look at God's fatherly care toward his undeserving people, see Hosea 11:1-4 (also Deuteronomy 33:27).

4 Read Psalm 18:1-19 and then answer the following questions:

- What titles does David use in referring to God? (vv.1-2)

- Who did David call when in trouble? (v.3, 6)

- Why does God rescue us? (v.19)

know what had happened. All went smoothly until I called my parents and my father answered the phone.

"Dad, we lost the baby. Clara had a miscarriage last night."

"Gee, Rob, I'm real sorry to hear that."

When he said those few words, simple and sincere, something broke and I burst into tears. I was surprised by the intensity of my weeping and how quickly it came over me. Then I realized that in the presence of my father, I didn't have to be in charge. I was free to release the emotion stored up inside me. I was able to be his son. Under the umbrella of our heavenly Father's protection we are free to be vulnerable and to express our deepest emotions. (Of course, it's also true that if the crying goes on too long, Dad will encourage you to "suck it up" and get on with business!)

There is a limitless amount of spiritual ore to be mined in the revelation of God as Father. And however much our earthly fathers may suggest divine qualities, they fall far, far short of our Father in heaven.

Looking Ahead to the Future

What prompted God to give us the incomparable privilege of membership in his family? Paul reaches back into eternity past to supply us with an answer: "For he chose us in him before the creation of the world to be holy and blameless in his sight. In love he predestined us to be adopted as his sons through Jesus Christ, in accordance with his pleasure and will" (Eph 1:4-5). It was God's love that brought about this great salvation. Rest assured that your own individual merit (or lack thereof) was never a factor. God, in the wonder of his love, decided to adopt you before the creation of the world.

> **❝** Those born once only, die twice. They die a temporal, and they die an eternal death. But those who are born twice, die only once; for over them the second death has no power.[13] **❞**
> — **William S. Plumer**

How comforting to know that God's choice of us had nothing to do with how attractive, clever, or good we are. If such were the case, he might be tempted to trade us in on a better model! We didn't earn adoption by our works and we don't keep it by works. Adoption is a gift of grace which originated in God's heart at the very beginning of time.

Looking back into eternity past provokes an outpouring of gratitude, but it's equally exciting to gaze into eternity future. We have yet to see the completion of all that adoption brings. Paul speaks for every Christian in expressing his great anticipation of the future: "We ourselves, who have the firstfruits of the Spirit, groan inwardly as we wait eagerly for our adoption as sons, the redemption of our bodies" (Ro 8:23).

Despite our current status as God's sons and daughters, our adoption won't be fully consummated until the day God redeems, or resurrects, our bodies. Few subjects have triggered as much speculation and excitement in the Church as this one. We all have a desire to understand what awaits us at the end of the age. Though to the natural mind these things are shrouded in mystery, Scripture provides us with the broad outlines of what we can expect to see take place.

---

5 Which of the following will signal the Lord's return? (Check all that apply)

❑ A trumpet blast and a shout

❑ A "Rapture Special" on used burial plots

❑ Resurrection of the righteous dead

❑ Abandoned homes, cars, and tennis shoes

❑ A reunion in the clouds

❑ The 77th Edition (Revised and Updated) of *Why The Rapture Will Take Place In...*

The Bible reveals that there are three stages of man's existence. First is the *natural state,* which spans the time from our conception to physical death. Body and soul are joined together. This is life as we know it in the present world. In spite of the fact that this state involves a great deal of cares and suffering, few of us are in a hurry to enter stage two—the *intermediate state.* This period stretches from the time of our death until the return of Jesus Christ and is characterized by a separation of the body from the soul or spirit (I'm using the terms interchangeably). The physical part of us reverts to dust while the immaterial part "returns to God who gave it" (Ecc 12:7). The spirits of all those who have died in Christ are currently with Christ. You won't find better accommodations than this. Paul, knowing he faced the very real prospect of death, made it clear that he found the intermediate state superior to the natural: "I am torn between the two: I desire to depart and be with Christ, which is better by far" (Php 1:23).

Meditate on
Ecclesiastes 3:11.
Where did our interest
in the future originate?

While hanging on the Cross, Jesus promised the penitent thief they would be together in paradise that very day (Lk 23:43). A comparison of this with 2 Corinthians 12:1-4 shows that "heaven," "paradise," and "being with Jesus" all refer to the same place. While in this intermediate state we will neither be unconscious ("soul sleep") nor will we be serving any stint in purgatory, both of which are unscriptural doctrines. We'll be instantly conformed to Jesus' image, our sanctification complete. No longer will we be troubled by the presence of sin. Best of all, we'll enjoy unbroken fellowship with the Lord. That's my only concern. As long as I'm with him, I'll have no anxiety about any unresolved details.

> **"** That we shall live again is surely no more wonderful or mysterious than that we are alive now. The real wonder rather would seem to be that after having not been in existence through an eternity that is past, we are now in existence...Surely it is far more incredible that from *not* having been, we are, than that from *actual being* we shall continue to be.[14] **"**
> — Loraine Boettner

As grand as this intermediate state will be, it is not the *final state* of our existence. The time is coming when "the trumpet shall sound, the dead will be raised and we shall be changed" (1Co 15:52). This is also known as *the glorified state* and will commence at the return of our Lord. On that day the dead will be raised and reunited with their glorified bodies. Once again it is Paul who depicts what this day will bring: "Our citizenship is in heaven. And we eagerly await a Savior from there, the Lord Jesus Christ, who, by the power that enables him to bring everything under his control, will transform our lowly bodies so that they will be like his glorious body" (Php 3:20, 21).

The longest chapter in any of Paul's letters, 1 Corinthians 15, focuses almost exclusively on our pending resurrection. He wrote the chapter in response to certain members of the Corinthian church who considered the resurrection unbelievable and unnecessary. Just in case we have any Corinthian tendencies, let's note the highlights of Paul's instruction in this chapter:

■ The resurrection is essential to Christianity. If you take away Jesus' resurrection, you remove the basis for forgiveness (vv.12-19).

■ Jesus Christ is the firstfruits of those who rise; his resurrection guarantees the resurrection of all those who are in Christ (vv.20-22).

■ Death, our last and greatest enemy, will be overcome through the resurrection. Because Jesus died and rose again, he is no longer subject to death. The same reality awaits those who are his. Though we all have a strong natural aversion to death, God's Word, Jesus' example, and the presence of the Holy Spirit are sufficient to shepherd us through even this dark, shadowy valley. Far from devouring the Christian, death itself is swallowed up by victory—the victory of Jesus Christ (vv.26, 54-56).

■ What will these glorified, resurrection bodies be like? Paul says they will bear some similarity to our present bodies but will also differ in significant ways. The relationship between an acorn and an oak tree may serve as a fitting metaphor to describe the difference. We can also gain insight from studying the post-resurrection appearances of Jesus. Our new bodies will be imperishable, powerful, glorious, and primarily spiritual in nature (vv.35-44).

6 Here's an abbreviated inventory of the things we must leave behind when we assume our glorified state. Check any items you would prefer to carry with you into eternity.

❏ Stress

❏ Excess weight

❏ Depression

❏ Sorrow and sighing

❏ Malfunctioning computers

❏ Taxes

❏ Acne

❏ Fear

❏ Sickness and disease

❏ Confusion about God's will

Be Done with Dross and Dung

Attempting to bring this final chapter to a close gives me a new sympathy for Paul, whose lengthy tributes to the grace and mercy of God made an art form of the run-on sentence. Where does one end? The doctrine of justification is unparalleled in scope and beauty. It's no coincidence that the four living creatures continually proclaim the Lord's holiness, and that with each declaration the twenty-four elders prostrate themselves in continuous worship before the glorified Lamb of God (Rev 4:8-11).

Jesus' parable about the wedding feast leaves us with just the right mix of celebration and sobriety (Mt 22:2-14). You are probably familiar with the story. A king was hosting a wedding banquet for his son, and sent invitations throughout his kingdom. When his honored guests rejected the invitation, however, the king refused to change his plans. "Go to the street corners and invite to the banquet anyone you find," he said. Soon the hall was filled. These lower-class guests weren't accustomed to royal etiquette, so it's likely that the king outfitted them with clothes befitting the occasion.

In the midst of the feasting the king entered the ban-

For Further Study:
Consider these words from an old folk hymn: "This world is not my home, I'm just a-passin' through." With that pilgrim mindset, read 2 Corinthians 5:1-5. Where was Paul's citizenship? Where is yours?

86

quet hall to see his guests, and it's here we find the crux of the parable: "But when the king came in he noticed a man there who was not wearing wedding clothes. 'Friend,' he asked, 'how did you get in here without wedding clothes?'"

In seeking to understand the king's indignation, some have conjectured that it was customary in Jesus' day for the host to provide his guests with wedding garments, especially guests of lesser means. This under-dressed guest wasn't an innocent victim of poverty; he had blatantly scorned the generous provision of his host.

> 66 The choicest portion of every Christian's existence is [yet] before him.[15] 99
> — William S. Plumer

Without hesitation the king ordered that he be bound hand and foot and cast out into the darkness.

God Almighty has rounded us up off the street corners and offered us a place at his Son's wedding feast. He has given us robes of righteousness to replace our filthy rags. A tremendous, eternal celebration is in store. But let's pay close attention to the dress code. Hand-sewn garments, no matter how painstakingly or diligently fashioned, will insult the Lord of the banquet. Only the free gift of justification, the finished work of our Lord Jesus Christ, can usher us into the favor and presence of God.

"Had I all the faith of the patriarchs," said one nineteenth-century saint, "all the zeal of the prophets, all the good works of the apostles, all the holy sufferings of the martyrs, and all the glowing devotion of the seraphs; I would disclaim the whole, in point of dependence, and count all but dross and dung, when set in competition with the infinitely precious death, and infinitely meritorious righteousness of the Lord Jesus Christ."[16] Delivered from God's wrath and justified by his grace, we've only just begun to comprehend the magnitude of this great salvation. But we still have a little time. An eternity, in fact—though even that may not be enough. ■

1. What is the best memory you have of your father?

2. Discuss the "angst" the author describes on page 78. How is this expressed in those who haven't been justified in Christ?

3. Discuss your reaction to the story about Renee's adoption on pages 78-79.

4. List three adjectives you think of when you hear the word "judge." How about the word "Father"?

5. Have you had bad experiences with your human father that make it difficult to draw near to your heavenly father?

6. "How comforting to know that God's choice of us had nothing to do with how attractive, clever, or good we are," writes the author (page 83). What then motivated him to adopt us?

7. Is there anything that would make you feel awkward referring to God in your prayers as "Daddy"?

8. How has your heavenly Father provided for you in the past week?

9. Which of the following best expresses your hope of future glory? A.) Can't wait! B.) Sounds nice C.) I'm not ready D.) A one-way flight to *where?*

10. Read Hebrews 11:13-16 aloud. What characterized the individuals mentioned here? How can we develop a similar desire?

RECOMMENDED READING *Immortality* by Loraine Boettner (Phillipsburg, NJ: Presbyterian and Reformed Publishing Company, 1984)

The Bible on the Life Hereafter by William Hendriksen (Grand Rapids, MI: Baker Book House, 1987)

The Atonement by Leon Morris (Downwers Grove, IL: InterVarsity Press, 1984)

The Glory of Christ by Peter Lewis (Chicago, IL: Moody Press, 1997)

NOTES **CHAPTER ONE** – This Great Salvation

1. Sinclair Ferguson, *The Christian Life: A Doctrinal Introduction* (Carlisle, PA: The Banner of Truth Trust, 1989), p. ix.
2. James Cantelon, *Theology for Non-Theologians* (New York: Macmillan Publishing, 1988), p. 6.
3. Sinclair Ferguson, *The Christian Life,* p. 2.
4. F.F. Bruce, *Tyndale New Testament Commentaries—Romans* (Grand Rapids, MI: Wm. B. Eerdmans Publishing Co., 1983), pp. 177–78.
5. James Cantelon, *Theology for Non-Theologians,* p. 101.
6. Jerry Bridges, *Trusting God* (Colorado Springs, CO: NavPress, 1988), p. 71.
7. Anthony Hoekema, *Saved By Grace* (Grand Rapids, MI: Wm. B. Eerdmans Publishing Co., 1989) p. 177.
8. F.F. Bruce, *Tyndale New Testament Commentaries—Romans,* p. 181.
9. Sinclair Ferguson, *The Christian Life,* p. 187.

CHAPTER TWO – Does Anyone Believe in Sin?

1. Thomas Greer, *A Brief History of the Western World, 5th Ed.* (San Diego, CA: Harcourt Brace Jovanovich Publishers, 1987), p. 378.
2. Karl Menninger, *Whatever Became of Sin?* (New York: Bantam Books, Inc., 1973), pp. 15–16.
3. James Buchanan, *The Doctrine of Justification* (Grand Rapids, MI: Baker Book House, 1867, 1955), p. 222.
4. John Bunyan from *Gathered Gold* (Hertfordshire, England: Evangelical Press, 1984), p. 291.
5. William Ernest Henley from *Bartlett's Familiar Quotations* (New York: Little, Brown, and Company, 1919), p. 829.
6. William S. Plumer, *The Grace of Christ* (Philadephia, PA: Presbyterian Board of Publication, 1853), p. 24.
7. J.C. Ryle, *Holiness* (Hertfordshire, England: Evangelical Press, 1879, 1979), p. 65.
8. R.C. Sproul, *Chosen By God* (Wheaton, IL: Tyndale House Publishers, 1986), pp. 97–98.
9. D. Martyn Lloyd-Jones, *Romans: Assurance, Chapter Five* (Grand Rapids, MI: Zondervan Publishing House, 1972), p. 219.
10. Donald MacLeod from *Gathered Gold* (Hertfordshire, England: Evangelical Press, 1984), p. 65.
11. William Plumer, *The Grace of Christ,* p. 20.
12. Jonathan Edwards, *The Works of Jonathan Edwards, Vol. 1* (Carlisle, PA: The Banner of Truth Trust, 1974), p. xlvii.
13. Ibid.
14. John MacArthur, Jr., *Our Sufficiency in Christ* (Dallas, TX: Word Publishing, 1991), p. 70.
15. J.C. Ryle, *Holiness,* p. 5.

CHAPTER THREE – The Holiness of God

1. Stephen Charnock, *The Existence and Attributes of God, Vol. II* (Grand Rapids, MI: Baker Book House, 1979 reprint), p. 112.
2. Henrietta Mears, *What the Bible Is All About* (Ventura, CA: Regal Books, 1983), p. 51.

3. T.C. Hammond, *In Understanding Be Men* (London, England: InterVarsity Fellowship, 1938).

4. Ibid., p. 58.

5. J.I. Packer, *Knowing God* (Downers Grove, IL: InterVarsity Press, 1973), p. 79.

6. R.C. Sproul, *The Holiness of God* (Wheaton, IL: Tyndale House Publishers, 1985), p. 164.

7. Ibid., pp. 45–46.

8. C.S. Lewis, *Mere Christianity* (New York: Macmillan Publishing Co., Inc., 1943), p. 38.

9. C.S. Lewis, *The Voyage of the "Dawn Treader"* (New York: Macmillan Publishing Co., Inc., 1952), p. 138.

10. Jonathan Edwards, "Sinners In the Hands of An Angry God."

11. Sinclair Ferguson, *A Heart for God* (Colorado Springs, CO: NavPress, 1985), p. 130.

12. J.C. Ryle, *Expository Thoughts on the Gospels: Luke* (Hertfordshire, England: Evangelical Press, 1879, 1985), p. 71.

13. Sinclair Ferguson, *A Heart for God,* p. 129.

CHAPTER FOUR – The Wrath of God

1. Peter T. O'Brien, *Word Biblical Commentary—Colossians, Philemon* (Waco, TX: Word Publishing Co., 1982), p. 66.

2. Bruce Milne, *Know the Truth* (Leicester, England: InterVarsity Press, 1982), p. 154.

3. R.C. Lucas, *The Message of Colossians and Philemon* (Downers Grove, IL: InterVarsity Press, 1980), p. 61.

4. Anthony Hoekema, *Saved by Grace* (Grand Rapids, MI: Wm. B. Eerdmans Co., 1989), p.47

5. From a tape by R.C. Sproul titled "Saved from the Wrath to Come" (Lake Mary, FL: Ligonier Ministries, 1991).

6. Bruce Milne, *Know the Truth*, p. 154.

7. From a tape by R.C. Sproul titled "The Innocent Native in Africa," from the series *Objections Answered* (Lake Mary, FL: Ligonier Ministries).

8. John R.W. Stott, *The Cross of Christ* (Downers Grove, IL: InterVarsity Press, 1986), p. 109.

9. Ibid.

10. Anthony Hoekema, *Saved by Grace* (Grand Rapids, MI: Wm. B. Eerdmans, 1989), p. 153.

11. John R.W. Stott, *The Cross of Christ,* p. 159.

12. Peter T. O'Brien, *Word Commentary—Colossians, Philemon,* p. 66.

CHAPTER FIVE – Justified by Christ

1. James Montgomery Boice, *Romans, Vol. I* (Grand Rapids, MI: Baker Book House, 1991), p. 380, 447.

2. Anthony Hoekema, *Saved by Grace* (Grand Rapids, MI: Wm. B. Eerdmans Co., 1989), p. 152.

3. Sinclair Ferguson, *The Christian Life: A Doctrinal Introduction* (Carlisle, PA: The Banner of Truth Trust, 1989), p. 80.

4. John R.W. Stott, *Only One Way: The Message of Galatians* (Downers Grove, IL: InterVarsity Press, 1968), p. 60.

5. Anthony Hoekema, *Saved by Grace,* p. 178.

6. John R.W. Stott, *Only One Way,* p. 59.

7. Sinclair Ferguson, *The Christian Life*, p. 72.
8. William S. Plumer, *The Grace of Christ* (Philadelphia, PA: Presbyterian Board of Publication, 1853), p. 195.
9. Alister McGrath, *Justification by Faith* (Grand Rapids, MI: Zondervan Publishing House, 1988), p. 132.
10. John R.W. Stott, *Only One Way*, p. 59.
11. Sinclair Ferguson, *The Christian Life*, p. 82–83.
12. Jerry Bridges, *Transforming Grace* (Colorado Springs, CO: NavPress, 1991), p. 98.
13. Sinclair Ferguson, *Grow in Grace* (Carlisle, PA: The Banner of Truth Trust, 1989), p. 56, 58–59.
14. J.I. Packer, *God's Words: Studies of Key Bible Themes* (Downers Grove, IL: InterVarsity Press, 1981), p. 147.
15. Timothy George, *Theology of the Reformers* (Nashville, TN: Broadman Press, 1988), p. 59.

CHAPTER SIX – The Fruits of Justification (I)

1. William S. Plumer, *The Grace of Christ* (Philadelphia, PA: Presbyterian Board of Publication, 1853), pp. 201–02.
2. Ibid., p. 230.
3. John R.W. Stott, *Men Made New* (Grand Rapids, MI: Baker Book House, 1966, 1991), pp. 9–10.
4. D. Martyn Lloyd-Jones, *Romans: Assurance, Chapter Five* (Grand Rapids, MI: Zondervan Publishing House, 1971), p. 10.
5. R.C. Sproul, *The Holiness of God* (Wheaton, IL: Tyndale House Publishers, 1985), p. 193.
6. Sinclair Ferguson, *Christian Spirituality (Reformed View)*, Donald Alexander, ed. (Downers Grove, IL: InterVarsity Press, 1988), p. 57.
7. Rebecca Pippert, *Hope Has Its Reasons* (New York: HarperCollins Publishers, Inc., 1989), pp. 102–104.
8. Oswald Chambers, *My Utmost for His Highest* (New York: Dodd, Mead & Company, 1963), p. 325.
9. John Owen, *Works, Vol. VI* (Carlisle, PA: The Banner of Truth Trust, 1967), p. 324.
10. John R.W. Stott, *Men Made New*, p. 30.
11. J.C. Ryle, *Holiness* (Hertfordshire, England: Evangelical Press, 1879, 1979), p. 29.
12. Sinclair Ferguson, *Christian Spirituality (Reformed View)*, p. 58.

CHAPTER SEVEN – The Fruits of Justification (II)

1. Edmund P. Clowney, *Preaching and Biblical Theology* (Phillipsburg, NJ: Presbyterian and Reformed Publishing Company, 1961), p. 15.
2. Gordon R. Lewis, *Confronting the Cults* (Grand Rapids, MI: Baker Book House, 1966), p. 25.
3. J.I. Packer, *Knowing God* (Downers Grove, IL: InterVarsity Press, 1973), p. 181.
4. Ibid.
5. W. v. Martitz, *Theological Dictionary of the New Testament, Vol. VIII*, G. Kittle and G. Friedrich, Eds. (Grand Rapids, MI: Wm. B. Eerdmans Publishing Co., 1972), p. 398.
6. William Hendrikson, *New Testament Commentary, Romans— Chapters 1–8* (Grand Rapids, MI: Baker Book House, 1980), p. 259.
7. Ibid.
8. Ibid.

9. F.F. Bruce, *Tyndale New Testament Commentary, Romans* (Grand Rapids, MI: Wm. B. Eerdmans Publishing Co., 1963), pp. 166–67.

10. William Hendrikson, *Romans Commentary,* p. 258.

11. D. Martyn Lloyd-Jones, *Romans: An Exposition of Chapter 8:5-17* (Grand Rapids, MI: Zondervan Publishing House, 1974), p. 243.

12. J.I. Packer, *Knowing God*, p. 188.

13. William S. Plumer, *The Grace of Christ* (Philadelphia, PA: Presbyterian Board of Publication, 1853), p. 266.

14. Loraine Boettner, *Immortality* (Phillipsburg, NJ: Presbyterian and Reformed Publishing House, 1956, 1984), p. 59.

15. William Plumer, *The Grace of Christ,* p. 404.

16. Ibid., p. 236–37.

OTHER TITLES IN THE *PURSUIT OF GODLINESS* SERIES

DISCIPLINES FOR LIFE
C.J. Mahaney and John Loftness

Are you satisfied with the depth of your devotional life? If you're like most Christians, probably not. *Disciplines for Life* puts change within your grasp. Leave the treadmill of spiritual drudgery behind as you discover fresh motivation and renewed passion to practice the spiritual disciplines. (96 pages)

HOW CAN I CHANGE?
C.J. Mahaney and Robin Boisvert

How Can I Change? (originally titled *From Glory to Glory*) rests on a remarkable assumption: If you will study and apply the doctrine of sanctification, any sin can be overcome. Have you known the frustration of falling short in your efforts to please God? Have you questioned whether you will *ever* be able to change? If so, this book can have a profound impact on your walk with Christ. (112 pages)

FIRST STEPS OF FAITH
Steve Shank

Other than a Bible, what's the first resource you would give a brand-new Christian? *First Steps of Faith* will meet that critical need. Using vivid, personal illustrations, Steve Shank lays a solid yet simple foundation for a lifetime of growth. Mature Christians will also find plenty of meat as they explore the attributes of God, our battle against indwelling sin, and much more. (112 pages)

WHY SMALL GROUPS?
C.J. Mahaney, General Editor

Not simply a how-to guide, this illuminating book starts by answering the all-important question of *why* a church needs small groups. The short answer? Because small groups are invaluable in helping us to "work out our salvation together" in practical, biblical ways. Specially developed for leaders and members of small groups alike, *Why Small Groups?* is loaded with insight, wisdom, and practical instruction. This book can help put you on the fast track to Christian maturity. (128 pages)

THE RICH SINGLE LIFE
Andrew Farmer, foreword by Joshua Harris

How do you live your life as a Christian single? Are you aiming at something better than just continually coping? God intends the season of your singleness to be one of great richness, focus, and fulfillment in him—a time when abundance joins hands with opportunity, and your identity in Christ emerges from undivided devotion to the Lord. While acknowledging the unique challenges the single life can pose, this book applies the truth and the heart of the Scripture in a way that is inspiring, encouraging, and practical. (176 pages)

ADDITIONAL RESOURCES FROM SOVEREIGN GRACE MINISTRIES

WORSHIP MUSIC
Since 1982, our ministry has published more than 300 songs, written by men and women in our family of churches, and intended to assist Christians in their worship of God. After several releases with major Christian labels, we began the Come & Worship series in 1997 (under our former name, PDI Music) as our primary means of releasing new songs to the Body of Christ. That mission continues under the new name of Sovereign Grace Music (effective September, 2002).

> *"Singing and knowing. Rejoicing and reasoning. Delight and doctrine. That's Sovereign Grace! It is so rare, and so needed … So sing on, Sovereign Grace! And whatever you do, don't stop studying and thinking and preaching about our great Savior."* — **author and pastor John Piper**

> *"These songs are vital, rich, and heart-probing ... [Sovereign Grace] music moves my heart to worship."* — ***Randy Alcorn, author of*** **Safely Home, Edge of Eternity, Deadline, Dominion, *and* Money, Possessions & Eternity**

> *"I grew up in church. I grew up singing praise songs. But honestly, I didn't learn to worship until I encountered songs like the ones from Sovereign Grace. Great music? Yes, but better yet, great truth. They're rooted in God's word, anchored to the cross, drenched in grace. They're the kinds of songs our generation is longing for—songs that exalt God, songs that leave us standing in awe of Him."* — ***Joshua Harris, author of*** **I Kissed Dating Goodbye, Boy Meets Girl, *and* Not Even a Hint**

AUDIO MESSAGES
Sovereign Grace produces audio series on a number of topics, ideal for personal and small-group application. Thousands have been evangelized, exhorted, encouraged, and instructed by these messages, first presented in local churches or at conferences such as the various Sovereign Grace conferences for pastors, worship leaders and worship teams, small-group leaders, and others. At the teaching section of our website you can review outlines to many of these messages (www.sovereigngraceministries.org/teaching). These products are available in CD and audiocassette formats.

For more information, please visit www.sovereigngraceministries.org
To order from the Sovereign Grace Store, visit www.sovereigngracestore.com

Sovereign Grace Ministries
7505 Muncaster Mill Road
Gaithersburg, MD 20877
info@sovgracemin.org
301-330-7400